Revelation
of the Magi

Revelation of the Magi

THE LOST TALE OF THE WISE MEN'S JOURNEY TO BETHLEHEM

Brent Landau

HarperOne
An Imprint of HarperCollinsPublishers

HarperOne

FIRST EDITION

Designed by Janet M. Evans

Library of Congress Cataloging-in-Publication Data
Revelation of the Magi. English.
   Revelation of the Magi: the lost tale of the Wise Men's journey to Bethlehem / [translated by] Brent Landau.—1st ed.
     p. cm.
   Includes bibliographical references.
   ISBN 978–0–06–194703–2
   1. Magi. I. Landau, Brent. II. Title.
   BT315.3R4813 2010
   232.92'3—dc22

                    2010004099

10 11 12 13 RRD(H) 10 9 8 7 6 5 4 3 2 1

To three wise women . . .

my grandmother,

Helen Mason,

who inspired me to study religion;

my mother,

Deborah Landau,

who inspired my love of reading;

and my wife,

Elizabeth Bangs,

who inspires me every day.

CONTENTS

Revelation
of the Magi

The Sages and the Star-Child

The Magi—usually known as the "Three Wise Men" or "Three Kings"—are easily the most famous of the visitors who appear at Jesus's birth in the Gospel accounts of the Christmas story. Whether or not one is a churchgoer, practically everyone has heard of them. Their bringing of gifts to the Christ child began a tradition that has linked them forever with the rite of holiday gift giving. Despite their great fame, however, there is only one short passage in the New Testament that tells of the Magi, and this account is remarkably vague about these figures. Found in the Gospel of Matthew, chapter 2, verses 1 through 12, it says this:

> Now when Jesus was born in Bethlehem of
> Judea in the days of Herod the king, behold,
> wise men from the East came to Jerusalem,
> saying, "Where is he who has been born king

of the Jews? For we have seen his star in the East, and have come to worship him." When Herod the king heard this, he was troubled, and all Jerusalem with him; and assembling all the chief priests and scribes of the people, he inquired of them where the Christ was to be born. They told him, "In Bethlehem of Judea; for so it is written by the prophet:

*'And you, O Bethlehem, in the land of Judah,
are by no means least among the rulers of Judah;
for from you shall come a ruler
who will govern my people Israel.'"*

Then Herod summoned the wise men secretly and ascertained from them what time the star appeared; and he sent them to Bethlehem, saying, "Go and search diligently for the child, and when you have found him bring me word, that I too may come and worship him." When they had heard the king they went their way; and lo, the star which they had seen in the East went before them, till it came to rest over the place where the child was. When they saw the star, they rejoiced exceedingly with great joy; and going into the house they saw the child with Mary his mother, and they fell down and worshiped him. Then, opening their treasures, they offered him gifts, gold and frankincense and myrrh. And being warned in a dream not to return to Herod, they departed to their own country by another way.

Notice the enormous gaps in this story, gaps that a thoughtful reader must attempt to fill in. The wise men have no specific country of origin. No number or names are given for the wise men, though three was destined to become the most common number because of the three gifts (See *The Three Kings [Wise Men]* on pages 4 and 5).[1]

In fact, "wise men" itself is a rather poor translation of the Greek word *magoi*,[2] which elsewhere in the New Testament means "magicians" in a clearly negative sense.[3] Equally problematic—if not altogether disturbing—is the puzzling nature of this "star" that the Magi have followed to Judea. The Gospel of Matthew never explains how the Magi came to know that this star revealed the birth of the King of the Jews. Moreover, the star itself behaves very strangely, reappearing to the Magi on their way to Bethlehem[4] and then coming to rest directly over the place where the child Jesus was. All in all, the story of the Magi from Matthew's Gospel is a very bizarre one, and many early Christians struggled to make sense of it.

+SCS BALTHASSAR +SCS ME

SCS CASPAR .

Sixth-century mosaic of the
Magi from Sant'Apollinare
Nuovo, Ravenna, Italy.
This mosaic demonstrates
some of the key features
of the early Christian
interpretation of the Magi
story: the number of the
Magi as three, their names,
and even their range of ages.

Amid a wide range of early Christian speculation on the Magi—apocryphal Gospels, hymns, sermons, mosaics, wood carvings, and sculptures on sarcophagi—one composition is particularly impressive and yet surprisingly unknown. Called the *Revelation of the Magi*, it is a lengthy narrative that claims to be the personal testimony of the Magi themselves on the events of Christ's coming. Though versions of this legend were well known in Christian Europe throughout the Middle Ages, this book presents the first-ever complete English translation of the *Revelation of the Magi*.

I confess that I have had a lifelong fascination with the Christmas holiday, with the traditions of Jesus's birth and childhood, and with the story of the Magi and their star in particular. As a young child, I was captivated when my church in Flagstaff, Arizona, brought in an astronomer from the nearby Lowell Observatory one Advent season to discuss the range of possible scientific explanations for the Star of Bethlehem. Then, during my high school education at a Jesuit school in Phoenix, I first learned about the existence of writings outside the New Testament that purported to fill in gaps in the Gospel accounts of Jesus's upbringing. Finally, as a doctoral student studying early Christianity at Harvard University, I was deeply impressed during a study trip to Italy when I saw how popular a subject the Magi were in paintings, altarpieces, and sculptures. Upon my return

to Cambridge, I resolved to learn as much as I could
about early Christian legends of the Magi. In this search,
I happened upon an article that mentioned the *Revelation of the Magi*. I asked around and was surprised to
find that none of my colleagues had even heard of it. Did
such a document really exist? It sounded like such a remarkable text that almost immediately I decided to in-
vestigate further.

7

Later in this introduction, I will discuss where this
text came from, why it is so little known today, and why
it may be a writing of great importance. But I'll start
with the contents of the story itself, which I eventually
discovered hidden away in the Vatican Library.

THE STORY

The *Revelation of the Magi*, mostly narrated by the Magi
in the first person, is a sweeping and imaginative work
that begins in the Garden of Eden and ends with the
Magi being baptized at the hands of the Apostle Thomas.
These Magi are members of an ancient mystical order
and reside in a semimythical land called Shir, located in
the extreme east of the world, at the shore of the Great
Ocean. The *Revelation of the Magi* says these individuals
are called "Magi" in the language of their country because they pray in silence. The story implies that the
name "Magi" is thus a play on the words *silence* and/or

prayer, but that implication does not make sense in any of the most common languages spoken by early Christians. Despite this unsolved mystery, however, this description sharply distinguishes the Magi of this story from any of the most common ancient usages of the term *magoi*: these Magi are not magicians, astrologers, or even priests of the Iranian religion of Zoroastrianism.[5]

These mystics, who live in a mysterious, far-off land, as the *Revelation of the Magi* depicts its Magi, are the descendants of Seth, the third son of Adam and Eve. Seth was believed by many early Jews and Christians to be extremely pious and virtuous, so it is very fitting for the *Revelation of the Magi* to trace the ancestry of the Magi back to such an illustrious founder. The Magi inherited from Seth a prophecy of supreme importance for the world: *a star of indescribable brightness will someday appear, heralding the birth of God in human form.* Seth himself had learned about this prophecy from his father, Adam, since the star originally had hovered over the Tree of Life, illumining all of Eden, before Adam's sin caused the star to vanish.

Every month of every year, for thousands of years, the order of the Magi has carried out its ancient rituals in expectation of this star's arrival. They ascend their country's most sacred mountain, the Mountain of Victories, and pray in silence at the mouth of the Cave of Treasures of Hidden Mysteries, where Seth's own prophetic books are housed and read by the Magi. Whenever one of the Magi dies, his son or one of his close relatives takes his place, and their order continues through the ages.

All of this lore about the origins of the Magi and their prophecy has been narrated, we are told, by the generation of the Magi that was alive to witness the coming of the star. They have gathered together to ascend the Mountain of Victories, as was their ancient custom, but suddenly the foretold star appears in the heavens. As promised, the star is indescribably bright, so bright that the sun becomes as faint as the daytime moon; yet because the Magi alone are worthy of guarding this prophecy, the star can be seen by no one but them. The star descends to the peak of the mountain and enters the Cave of Treasures, bidding the Magi to come inside. The Magi enter the cave and bow before the star, whose incredible light gradually dissipates to reveal *a small, luminous human!* This "star-child" reveals to the Magi that he is the Son of God, but—and this is of crucial importance—never calls himself by the familiar names *Jesus* or *Christ*. Nor do the Magi themselves ever call him by these names, and the absence of these designations will provide us with a critical clue about the central message of the *Revelation of the Magi*.

The star-child instructs the Magi to follow it to Jerusalem so that they may witness its birth and participate in the salvation God has planned for the entire world.

The Magi descend from the mountain, discussing excitedly what they have just seen. In the course of their conversation, however, they learn that *each of them saw the star-child in a different form, with each vision representing a different time in the life of Christ!* They prepare a caravan and supplies for the lengthy trek, but thanks to the overwhelming power of the star, their journey proves to be truly extraordinary. The star removes any and all obstacles from their path, leveling valleys and mountains, making rivers passable on foot, and protecting the Magi from wild animals. The star's light also relieves the Magi of their fatigue and continuously refills their food supplies. For the Magi, this vast journey from the eastern edge of the world to the land of Judea seems to have transpired in the mere blink of an eye.

10

The star leads the Magi into Jerusalem, where the city's inhabitants puzzle at these exotic foreigners. Because the star is invisible to the inhabitants, they presume these visitors to be astrologers of some kind, since the Magi keep looking up at the heavens. The Magi's encounter with Herod and the Jewish religious leaders in Jerusalem unfolds almost identically to the narrative of Matthew's Gospel—one of the rare times that the *Revelation of the Magi* closely follows the story line of Matthew.

Immediately after the Magi hear the Jewish prophecy about the birth of the Messiah at Bethlehem, the star reappears to the them[6] and leads them to a cave in the environs of the village. Just as upon the Mountain of Victories, the star enters the cave and beckons the Magi inside. Here the star transforms into a luminous, talking infant, whose "birth" is accompanied by unseen angels singing his praises. In a lengthy speech, the infant tells the Magi that their ancient mysteries have at last been fulfilled and commissions them to become witnesses to him and his Gospel for the people of their homeland.

As the Magi exit the Bethlehem cave, rejoicing at the fulfillment of their ancient prophecy, they are met by Mary and Joseph, who have suddenly appeared on the scene. In a very odd exchange, Mary accuses them of trying to steal her newborn infant, but the Magi assuage her concern by explaining that the child is actually the savior of the world and can be in many places simultaneously.

The Magi then begin their journey back to Shir, a trip that, through the awesome power of the star, transpires for them as quickly as did their travel to Bethlehem. The star's light refills their food supplies even more abundantly than before, and when the Magi eat of these provisions, they again see their guide in a multitude of different forms. When they reach the borders of their homeland, crowds of their family members and kinspeople come out to meet them, marveling at the appearance and health of the travelers. The Magi relate the story of their miraculous encounter with the star and subsequent journey to the people of Shir. They conclude their story by revealing to the people that they, too, can come to experience the presence of the star-child, whom the Magi claim is still with them—since he is, in fact, present throughout the entire world. The Magi present the people with the overflowing bags of food that the star has produced for them and invite them to partake. Those people who eat immediately see visions of the heavenly and earthly Christ, and thus many in the land of Shir accept the faith proclaimed by the Magi.

Thus far, the Magi's age-old prophecy has been fulfilled: they have journeyed with the star, witnessed the birth of Christ, preached his Gospel to their kinspeople, and now remain in the light of Christ's eternal presence. This would seem like a most fitting and fulfilling way for this story to conclude, yet the only copy of the *Revelation of the Magi* that we possess does not end here. In a concluding episode that may not have been part of the original story (more on the reasons for this later), the Apostle Thomas comes to the homeland of the Magi on a missionary journey—presumably after many years have passed. The Magi hear of his arrival and come to meet him, telling him of their experience of Christ's coming. Thomas recognizes that they have indeed had contact with Christ, and he relates to them his own memories of the ministry of Jesus. The Magi rejoice at what Thomas has said, and they ask him to initiate them into the Christian fellowship. When Thomas baptizes them early on Sunday morning, the heavenly Christ descends and administers the Eucharist, first to the apostle and then to the Magi. Thomas then commissions the Magi to proclaim the Gospel throughout the world, and the *Revelation of the Magi* ends with the Magi performing miracles and preaching.

FIRST IMPRESSIONS

Not only does the *Revelation of the Magi* have the distinction of being the most substantial early Christian composition about the Magi; its narrative complexity matches almost *any* early Christian writing. Thus, the first thing that one notices about the *Revelation of the Magi* is that whoever wrote it devoted a great deal of time and thought to crafting a rich and intricate story line. As a scholar of early Christian writings, I noticed several other surprising features immediately. Its location of the Magi in the far-eastern land of Shir was highly unusual, since most early Christians thought that the Magi came from Persia, Babylon, or Arabia (see *Adoration of the Magi* on page 14).

Also surprising was its identification of the Star of Bethlehem with Christ himself, an interpretation found nowhere else in the diverse array of early Christian

A wooden door carving of the adoration of
the Magi from the Basilica of Santa Sabina
in Rome. Like the mosaic from Ravenna, this
carving portrays the Magi wearing distinctive
"Phrygian caps," reflecting a belief that the
Magi are Zoroastrians from the land of Persia.

speculation about this mysterious celestial portent. The late entry of the Apostle Thomas into the action of narrative was quite unexpected, and raised a new series of questions for me about the relationship between the *Revelation of the Magi* and other texts that discuss the Apostle Thomas. I was also captivated by the very strange incident of the food that produced visions of Christ for the Magi and the people of Shir, given its parallels to the use of hallucinogenic substances in other religious traditions.

But finally and most importantly, I was surprised that neither I nor any of my colleagues knew of this impressive text's existence before I stumbled across a mention of it in an article. There are certainly a significant number of early Christian apocryphal writings that are familiar only to scholars specializing in apocryphal literature, but the *Revelation of the Magi* was completely unknown to me and to other specialists in this field that I consulted. For me as a doctoral student, such a poorly known text represented a wonderful opportunity to bring an important document into the mainstream of early Christian scholarship. Yet it would also prove to be a serious challenge to my skills as a researcher, since even basic questions about when and under what circumstances it was written were unresolved.

WHERE DID THE
"REVELATION OF THE MAGI" COME FROM?

As I mentioned earlier, the *Revelation of the Magi* has never before been translated into English, and very few specialists in early Christian apocryphal literature even know of its existence. How did this remarkable text come to be so neglected? Part of the problem is that the only known copy of the text is preserved in Syriac, a language used by ancient Christians throughout the Middle East and Asia, but one in which only a relatively small number of early Christian scholars are fluent. By comparison, many more scholars know Coptic, an Egyptian language in which such important texts as the Gospel of Thomas, the Gospel of Mary, and the Gospel of Judas have been preserved.

Another important reason for this text's neglect, however, is that it belongs to two categories of material that historically have been scorned in the study of early Christianity. First, it is an apocryphal writing, and scholars have long privileged the canonical writings of the New Testament to the exclusion of writings outside of the canon. There are, of course, a few exceptions, such as the writings just mentioned, but beyond these, most apocryphal writings remain sorely neglected.

Second, the *Revelation of the Magi* is one of a handful of canonical and apocryphal texts that focus on events surrounding the birth of Jesus. Although the Christmas story has fascinated believers throughout the centuries, there are only two accounts of Jesus's birth among the four canonical Gospels, suggesting that the birth of Jesus was not nearly as important for the first Christians as the death, Resurrection, and teachings of Jesus of Nazareth. Furthermore, Matthew and Luke tell markedly different stories about Jesus's birth, and the differences cannot be easily harmonized.[7] As a result, the great majority of scholars today believe that this material has very little claim to historicity and have therefore ignored it. The study of the historical Jesus has mostly focused on his sayings and his final days in Jerusalem; only a few recent scholars have found any reliable historical details in the infancy narratives—and the story of the Magi is not one of them.[8]

17

Even if it is poorly known today, the manuscript that contains the *Revelation of the Magi* was never truly lost—certainly not in the way that, say, the Dead Sea Scrolls were. After the existing manuscript was copied down at the Zuqnin monastery in southeastern Turkey by an anonymous monk at the end of the eighth century, it changed hands at some point and was kept in a monastery in the Egyptian desert. There it stayed until the eighteenth century, when G. S. Assemani, collecting manuscripts on behalf of the Vatican Library, brought it to Rome, where it resides today.

Though this manuscript had been known by European scholars for several hundred years, it was not until rather recently that scholars first began to look closely at the legend of the Magi that it contained. An Italian translation of the *Revelation of the Magi* was made in the 1950s, and a few scholars in the decades since have discussed the text in journal articles, often peripherally. Quite serendipitously, when I first learned of the existence of the *Revelation of the Magi,* I had just finished my first year of studying the Syriac language. I was therefore well prepared to begin translating the text with the help of J. F. Coakley, Professor of Syriac at Harvard.

After nearly a year of biweekly meetings with Professor Coakley to check my work, I had managed to produce a rough but complete translation of the *Revelation of the Magi.* Despite the many hours of work that this had required, my task as a scholar of early Christian writings was only beginning. Unlike a scholar working on a New Testament text or even a well-known apocryphal writing, there was virtually no preexisting "conversation" about the *Revelation of the Magi* into which I was entering. Very few scholars knew that the text existed at all, so there were only some tentative suggestions about how old the *Revelation of the Magi* might be, who might have written it, and where it was composed.[9]

To figure out the most likely date of composition, my first step was to start with the *latest* possible time the text could have been written and then work backward as far as possible. As mentioned earlier, there is only one copy of the *Revelation of the Magi* in existence, and that manuscript is securely dated to the late eighth century. Is it possible that the anonymous scribe who wrote this manuscript was actually the author of the *Revelation of the Magi?* Not likely, for several reasons. First, as a general matter, scholars of early Christianity know that the date of a manuscript is very rarely the date of the text it contains.[10] Second, the manuscript itself—known as the *Chronicle of Zuqnin,* for the monastery in which it was written—contains a number of writings that are known to have existed much earlier than the eighth century. Third, a Christian writer named Theodore bar Konai, who lived on the Arabian Peninsula at almost the same time that the chronicle was written, seems to have known about the *Revelation of the Magi.*[11] There is no reason to suspect that the *Chronicle of Zuqnin* would have traveled from southeastern Turkey to the Arabian Desert in the span of only a few years. It seems far more likely that the *Revelation of the Magi* was written—and circulated rather widely—earlier than the eighth century.

But how much earlier? Fortunately, even though we possess only one full copy of the *Revelation of the Magi,* there is another very important witness to this text. This other witness is a Latin commentary on the Gospel of Matthew, usually thought to have been written in the fifth century and known by scholars as the *Opus Imper-fectum in Matthaeum*. The anonymous writer of this commentary, when he comes to Matthew's story of the Magi, relates a legend about these mysterious figures. Even though he summarizes this legend in only a few short paragraphs, it is clearly the same story as that found in the *Revelation of the Magi*.[12] Moreover, it is very likely that he had actually seen a written copy of the *Revelation of the Magi*, since there are several parts of his summary that agree, practically verbatim, with the copy of the *Revelation of the Magi* that has survived for us.[13]

So it seems certain that a version of the *Revelation of the Magi* existed when the *Opus Imperfectum* was written in the fifth century. But how do we know that the Syriac text of the *Revelation of the Magi* that we have was written earlier than the fifth century? After all, it *could* be a later form of the legend that had been expanded significantly. There is one small, seemingly insignificant detail in the Syriac text that tells us when it was written. In the Syriac language, nouns can be either masculine or feminine, and in the *Revelation of the Magi*, "the Holy Spirit" is a feminine noun. Although it might surprise us today to think of the Holy Spirit as a female entity, this is exactly what Syriac writers of the second, third, and fourth centuries considered it/her. Starting in the fifth century, however, Syriac writers began to treat "the Holy Spirit" as a masculine noun, under influence from Greek Christian thought. What this means, therefore, is that *the Syriac language itself* confirms that the form of the *Revelation of the Magi* that we possess must have been written earlier than the fifth century.

But this quirk of the Syriac language tells us only that the text must have been written earlier than the fifth century. To determine how much earlier it was written, we need to look for other clues in the Syriac form of the *Revelation of the Magi*. Recall that in the summary of the *Revelation of the Magi* presented earlier, I suggested that the story of the Apostle Thomas's conversion of the Magi was probably not originally part of the *Revelation of the Magi*. Not only does it seem superfluous from a narrative point of view, but it also has a number of literary features that do not fit very well with what has come before. First, the Thomas episode is narrated in the third person, whereas the rest of the *Revelation of the Magi* is narrated by the Magi themselves, in the first person. Although such shifts in the perspective of the narrator are not unheard of in ancient Christian writings, this shift is especially abrupt and unexplained within the narrative. Second, the Thomas episode contains a striking change in terminology as compared with the first-person section of the *Revelation of the Magi*. One of the most distinctive features of the first-person section is its complete avoidance of the proper name "Jesus Christ" to refer to the divine being whom the Magi encounter. Yet as careful as the author is to forgo this name and other obviously Christian terminology, the Thomas section is not at all concerned to avoid the name "Jesus Christ," using it almost twenty times!

Because of these reasons, I believe that the Thomas episode was a later addition to the *Revelation of the Magi*. I will say more shortly about the reasons that someone might have wanted to tamper with a text that purported to be the authentic testimony of the Magi about the coming of Christ. But for now, let us use the Thomas episode to help find out more about when the *Revelation of the Magi* was written—or at least when it was tampered with. As it happens, stories about the Apostle Thomas were especially popular among ancient Christians living in Syria. The most famous collection of these stories is known as the Apocryphal Acts of the Apostle Thomas, and it includes accounts of his miracles, his preaching, and his eventual martyrdom in India. Even though the Acts of Thomas and the Thomas episode from the *Revelation of the Magi* do not tell the same story, they share numerous connections in their language and theology.[14] These similarities suggest that the Thomas episode was probably composed and added to the *Revelation of the Magi* around the same time and place as other Thomas legends were being written down—that is, around the late third or early fourth century in Syria. Therefore, the first-person form of the *Revelation of the Magi* must have been composed by this time *at the latest*,[15] and perhaps earlier if it came from someplace outside of Syria.

But how much earlier might the original form of the *Revelation of the Magi* have been written? Might it be, as it claims, the authentic testimony of the Magi themselves? As tantalizing a possibility as this might be, it is highly unlikely. First of all, there is the basic problem of historicity with the whole Magi story found in Matthew's Gospel. As mentioned earlier, scholars have by and large concluded that there is virtually nothing of historical value in the infancy narratives of the New Testament. This judgment has been applied with particular vigor to the Magi story.[16] Even the Star of Bethlehem, the most impressive feature of the story, has never been incontrovertibly identified, arguments to the contrary notwithstanding.[17] And the fact that no trace of the Magi story is found in Luke's infancy narrative, which has the humble shepherds as the first outside witnesses to the child Jesus, or in any other of the earliest Christian writings does not enhance its credibility.

But even if we were to grant that Matthew's story of the Magi was based on an actual historical event, the *Revelation of the Magi* would not be a very strong candidate to have been written by the Magi themselves. True, the author of the *Revelation of the Magi* has carefully crafted this story and added levels of detail such that one might *believe* it to be the work of the Magi themselves. Once we closely inspect the story, however, it becomes clear that the author has used written sources—such as the letters of the Apostle Paul, the Gospel of John, and the Book of Revelation, to name a few—that were written years after the "historical Magi" almost certainly would have died.[18]

In fact, the author not only used many of the earliest Christian writings in the New Testament. He seems to have used a rather obscure apocryphal Infancy Gospel that was likely written in the mid- to late-second century, a Gospel so obscure that it lacks an agreed-upon name![19] For the sake of (some) clarity, let us call it *Infancy Gospel X*.[20] In *Infancy Gospel X*, the Magi come to visit the child Jesus at a small house outside the village of Bethlehem. Joseph—the main actor in *Infancy Gospel X*, as opposed to the narratives in Matthew and Luke, where he never says a word—proceeds to question these strange visitors about how they knew of the child's birth.

During the ensuing dialogue with Joseph, the Magi mention a number of details corroborated by the *Revelation of the Magi*. These include learning of the star's coming through their own very ancient writings, the Magi's lack of fatigue after a lengthy journey, and the indescribably bright star being visible to the Magi alone. Joseph even presumes the Magi to be astrologers because they keep looking up at the sky, apparently watching their invisible celestial guide. A very similar scene takes place in the *Revelation of the Magi*, but there it is the leaders in Jerusalem, not Joseph, who cannot see the star. Finally, *Infancy Gospel X* envisions the Magi not as three in number, but as a much larger group—an interpretation hinted at in the *Revelation of the Magi* (see *The Adoration of the Magi* on page 27).[21]

These parallels are very striking, but in *Infancy Gospel X* all these details are tightly concentrated in the Magi's brief appearance at the Bethlehem cave, not spread throughout the narrative as in the *Revelation of the Magi*. It seems quite probable that there is some sort of literary relationship between these two works, but who has borrowed from whom? It is very difficult to tell, and it is even possible that the authors of these two works used a third source (whether oral or written) independently of each other. I myself have gone back and forth many times about which writing was older. More research on *Infancy Gospel X* would be necessary before a decisive judgment could be made.

Even so, if we assume that the *Revelation of the Magi* came into being sometime after *Infancy Gospel X*, then it was probably written in the late second or early third century. It was then "corrected" in the late third or early fourth century by adding the concluding narrative about the Apostle Thomas's visit to the Magi.

If the *Revelation of the Magi* was not, as it claims, written by the Magi themselves, then who might have written this strange story? Although it is possible to give, with a reasonable degree of confidence, a window of time during which it was composed, we have almost nothing to go on regarding the author's identity or location. Only a small number of early Christian writings are written by the person put forth as the author anyway, so the *Revelation of the Magi* is not much different from them in this respect.[22] The place of authorship is similarly unknowable: presumably the author's sophisticated theology—which we will address momentarily—suggests an urban location, perhaps Rome, Alexandria, Antioch, Ephesus, or another major urban center of the Roman world. All we know is that the *Revelation of the Magi* was known in Constantinople (where the author of the *Opus Imperfectum* found it) in the fifth century, and in southeastern Turkey (where an anonymous monk at the Zuqnin monastery copied it) and the Arabian Peninsula (where Theodore bar Konai lived) by the end of the eighth century.

Yet even if we cannot say much of anything substantial about the identity of the author or his whereabouts, we can actually say quite a bit about his understanding of the Christian message, and about why his understanding might have been viewed as theologically dangerous enough to warrant a new ending for the *Revelation of the Magi*.[23]

The Adoration of the Magi, by Benozzo Gozzoli,
1459, Florence, Italy. Gozzoli has not depicted
the familiar three Magi traveling alone, but
instead accompanied by a great cavalcade.
Both *Infancy Gospel X* and an early form of
the *Revelation of the Magi* likewise believed
that the Magi constituted a large group.

WHY WAS THE
"REVELATION OF THE MAGI" WRITTEN?

As mentioned earlier, one of the most noticeable features of the *Revelation of the Magi* is its careful avoidance of the name "Jesus Christ" to designate the Magi's celestial guide. This consistent omission is one of the reasons that the Apostle Thomas episode's free use of the name seems so jarring. Why has the author refused to use the name "Jesus Christ?" If the Magi in the first-person narrative come to the end of the story without ever using the name, this implies that they have had an experience of Christ without ever knowing this savior figure *as* Christ. The case of the Magi, then, raises the possibility that Christ has appeared to many people and yet not revealed himself *as* Jesus Christ.

The idea of Christ remaining unidentified in manifestations to the peoples of the world is, in fact, affirmed by statements that the celestial Christ makes to the Magi. He tells them that he has appeared not only to them in a manner congruent with their religion. Indeed, this is only one of many instances of Christ's revelation to humanity, since he has been sent "to fulfill everything that was spoken about me in the entire world and in every land" (13:10). Having heard this revelation from Christ, the Magi themselves then affirm it before others. To the inhabitants of Jerusalem, they explain that they have come to worship Christ "because he has worshipers in every land" (17:5). Even to the child's mother, Mary, they insist on the universality and omnipresence of the Christ event: "[T]he forms with him are seen in every land, because he has been sent by his majesty for the salvation and redemption of every human being" (23:4).

According to the author of the *Revelation of the Magi*, the fundamental Christian message is not simply that Christ has been sent in order to save all humanity. That is a common enough belief among early Christians that its presence in this text would be unremarkable. The *Revelation of the Magi* goes much further than this, claiming that *the revelation of Christ is actually the foundation of* all *humanity's religious beliefs and practices.* What the Magi have experienced in the fulfillment of their age-old prophecy, while obviously of great significance for them, is but "one drop of salvation from the house of majesty" (15:1)—one limited instance of Christ's salvific activity in the world.

What are the practical consequences of this belief that all forms of religious experience are revelations of Christ? Two especially come to mind. First, this belief means that the *Revelation of the Magi* has a far more positive view of non-Christian religious traditions than any other early Christian writing. There were a handful of early Christian thinkers who held that glimpses of

Christ were had in the past by the greatest of the pagan philosophers—Socrates, to name one example. But these thinkers also maintained that such glimpses were woefully incomplete when compared with the definitive revelation of Christ in the person of Jesus of Nazareth. And such an opinion, it must be remembered, is quite charitable when compared with most early Christian beliefs about non-Christian religions. The vast majority of early Christians, like their Israelite forebears, tended to regard the gods of other peoples as illusory at best, demonic at worst.

A second consequence of the *Revelation of the Magi*'s opinion about Christ's all-encompassing revelation is that it renders the traditional model of Christian expansion completely pointless. Throughout much of Christian history, and particularly since the beginning of the Age of Exploration in the fifteenth century, one dominant means by which Christianity has spread among non-Christian populations is through the work of dedicated missionaries. The general assumption is that the work of missionaries has been absolutely necessary because Jesus Christ delegated this task to the most devoted of his followers.[24]

But why could not Christ *himself* have been the principal agent of Christian expansion? If Christ existed before Jesus of Nazareth did (as the first verses of the Gospel of John claim) and could even visit people after his ascension (as Acts of the Apostles claims that he did to the Apostle Paul), then what would prevent Christ from appearing to *anyone,* in any place, at any time? This appears to have been a question asked by the author of the *Revelation of the Magi,* and his answer was, "Nothing." Christ appeared to the Magi before he assumed human flesh, and what is more, he apparently felt no need to identify himself to the Magi as Christ. The author, to be sure, is very concerned that the Christian revelation be spread to all the people of the world, but in his estimation, human missionaries are in no way essential for this task.

If we see this view of Christ as central to the author of the *Revelation of the Magi,* then it becomes much clearer why someone else would have felt compelled to change the original ending of the story. As the *Revelation of the Magi* originally ended, the Magi and the people of Shir have all come to experience the presence of Christ, though they have done so completely without any of the trappings that we might associate with institutional Christianity. They are, in the words of the great twentieth-century Catholic theologian Karl Rahner, "anonymous Christians." The Apostle Thomas episode solves this "problem" by having the Magi baptized and commissioned by an apostolic emissary to go preach the Gospel throughout the entire world.

A helpful analogy for what has happened to the *Revelation of the Magi* would be the difference between the "abrupt ending" and the "longer ending" of the Gospel of Mark, most likely the first of the canonical Gospels to be written. The vast majority of scholars today believe that the original ending of Mark's Gospel was at 16:8. This would mean that Mark ended with the women running terrified from the angel's appearance at the empty tomb of Jesus—that is, without any appearances of the resurrected Jesus. Mark would therefore have ended with the words "they said nothing to anyone, for they were afraid." Although the precise reasons for the "abrupt ending" will likely never be completely clear, some scholars believe that by it Mark intended to convey a powerful theological message to his audience—possibly that Christian faith grows and perseveres *in spite of* the frailty and often failure of its would-be messengers.

A powerful theological message, and arguably a brilliant ending to this Gospel. But also one that could be misunderstood or seem rather inadequate, particularly given the presence of Resurrection appearances in later Gospels. So someone, probably in the second century, attached a "longer ending" to Mark's Gospel (16:9–20) that contained several appearances of the risen Jesus, along with Jesus's missionary charge to his disciples. In other words, this individual changed the ending of Mark's Gospel to reflect much more clearly and explicitly how Christians in his time and place expected a Gospel to end. Something much like that seems to have happened to the *Revelation of the Magi*. It was simply not good enough for the Magi to have had a revelation of Christ that did not "make them Christians" in a straightforward and unambiguous way,[25] just as it was not good enough for the women of Mark's Gospel to hear that Jesus had been raised without *seeing* any definitive evidence of it or telling anyone about what they saw at the tomb. Hence, the endings of both Mark's Gospel and the *Revelation of the Magi* were rewritten and expanded to make them more palatable to the typical expectations of later Christians.

So, the *Revelation of the Magi* has a view of other religious traditions that is highly unusual among early Christian writings. That feature, along with its status as the longest and most developed apocryphal narrative about the Magi, should make it of considerable interest for scholars of Christian origins. But the present book would not have been written were *Revelation of the Magi* of interest for only a limited number of academic specialists. Over the past several years I have shared my work on this writing, with members of several church communities and with a number of friends and relatives, some of whom do not consider themselves especially religious. Their enthusiastic response, I believe, has much to do with the way in which the Magi have embedded themselves in popular culture to a degree surpassing many other figures from the Bible. Fewer and fewer people may have much understanding of such a monumental personality as, say, the Apostle Paul, but it seems as if *everyone* knows the wise men!

The *Revelation of the Magi* is indeed a fascinating and imaginative story about some of the Bible's most intriguing figures. But the emphasis of the *Revelation of the Magi* on the universality of Christ's revelation may also captivate many readers. The questions this writing poses are of potential importance for anyone who considers herself or himself religious, spiritual, or simply interested in theological questions. Could Christ actually be the source of multiple revelations throughout human history? Would there be any way of knowing this? What would the implications of this be for Christian attitudes toward non-Christian religions? What would this mean for the practice of evangelism? Would it even be correct to regard such a divine being as "Christ" if the Christian revelation is but a single isolated example of this being's salvific activity? Does any revelation take precedence over others? The answers to these questions will probably differ depending on one's basic religious convictions. But whether one is a born-again Christian, a Latter-day Saint, a "religious seeker," or a Buddhist, the *Revelation of the Magi* raises challenging questions about divine revelation, religious pluralism, and the uniqueness of religions—questions that merit deep, sustained reflection.

The English Translation of the "Revelation of the Magi"[26]

1. Introduction[27]

[1:1]About the revelation of the Magi, and about their coming to Jerusalem, and about the gifts that they brought to Christ.[28] [1:2]An account of the revelations and the visions, which the kings,[29] [sons of kings,[30]] of the great East[31] spoke,[32] who were called Magi in the language of that land because in silence, without a sound, they glorified and they prayed.[33] [1:3]And in silence and in the mind they glorified and prayed to the exalted and holy majesty of the Lord of life,[34] to the holy and glorious Father, who is hidden by the great brightness of himself and is more lofty and holy than all reasoning. [1:4]And the language of human beings is not able to speak about him as he is, except as he has wished, and when he has wished, and by means of whom he wishes. [1:5]And neither his heavenly worlds nor the lower ones are able to speak about his majesty, except as it is fitting for the will of his majesty to reveal to the worlds so that they are able to partake from the gift[35] of his majesty, because (his majesty) is great and they are not able to speak of it.

2. THE MAGI—THEIR NAMES AND LINEAGE

[2:1]And so, there were those wise men,[36] who were called Magi in the language of the land because in silence, without a sound, they praised the God of all, that one who, by his word and will, has come to be all that is, all that exists and arises, and all that is going to be. [2:2]And there is nothing that exists outside of his will,[37] and furthermore, there is no one who will stand against the will of the Father of all. [2:3]The names of the wise men and kings were called as follows:[38] Zaharwandad son of Artaban; Hôrmizd son of Sanatruq; Auštazp son of Gudaphar;[39] Aršak son of Mihruq; Zarwand son of Wadwad; Arîhô son of Kosrau; Artahšišat son of Hawîlat; Aštanbôzan son of Šîšrawan; Mihruq son of Humam; Ahširaš son of Sahban; Nasardîh son of Baladan; Merôdak son of Bîl. [2:4]These are kings, sons of Eastern kings, in the land of Shir,[40] which is the outer part of the entire East of the world inhabited by human beings, at the Ocean,[41] the great sea beyond the world, east[42] of the land of Nod,[43] that place in which dwelt Adam, head and chief of all the families of the world. [2:5]And these sons of kings received commandments, laws, and even books from their fathers.

²:⁶And generation from generation, one by one, they received (them,) from the time of Seth, the son of our father Adam, because Adam revealed (them) to his son Seth when he had him.⁴⁴ ²:⁷And Adam taught Seth about his prior greatness, before he transgressed against the commandment, and about his expulsion from Paradise.⁴⁵ And he warned his son Seth not to transgress also against the (divine) justice as Adam (did).

37

3. THE TRANSMISSION OF THE MYSTERIES

³:¹And Seth received the commandment of his father with a pure heart,⁴⁶ and he took care of the agreement and the gift of the exalted Lord of majesty. ³:²And it was given to Seth to set down in a book and to make known the wisdom, and to call upon the name of the LORD,⁴⁷ the Lord of every soul who seeks after life. ³:³And from him a book appeared in the world for the first time,⁴⁸ which was set down in the name of the Exalted One. ³:⁴And Seth entrusted to his descendants the book that was set down, and it was transmitted up to Noah, that one who was found just and was delivered from the waters.⁴⁹ ³:⁵And [in the time of the Deluge,] Noah [took] the books of commandments with him [in the Ark. And when] he came out of the Ark, Noah also commanded the generations after him, who recounted his great deeds and the hidden mysteries⁵⁰ that are written in the books of Seth about the

majesty of the Father and all the mysteries. [3:6]And the [books,] and the mysteries, and the speech were handed down in succession by tradition even until our [51] fathers. [3:7]And they learned and received with joy, and handed them down to us ourselves, and we also kept with love and fear their mysteries of the books and the secrets and the words. [3:8]And we prayed in silence and gave thanks and glorified, bowing our knees and lifting our hands to the height of heaven,[52] to the Lord of that majesty that is hidden from the eyes of everything that lives.

38

4. THE PROPHECY OF THE STAR

[4:1]And those books of hidden mysteries were placed on the Mountain of Victories[53] in the east of Shir, our country, in a cave, the Cave of Treasures of the Mysteries of the Life of Silence.[54] [4:2]And our fathers commanded us as they also received from their fathers, and they said to us:[55] "Wait for the light that shines forth to you from the exalted East[56] of the majesty of the Father, the light that shines forth from on high in the form of a star[57] over the Mountain of Victories and comes to rest upon a pillar of light[58] within the Cave of Treasures [of] Hidden Mysteries. [4:3]And also command your sons, and your sons their sons, until the mystery of the star that shines forth from the exalted majesty appears to your generations, a light like a star, and giving light to the entire creation and obscuring the light of the sun, moon, and stars, and not one of them is seen or is able to stand in the presence of its light.[59] [4:4]For it is the great mystery of the Son of the exalted majesty, who is the voice of the Father; the offspring of his hidden thought; the light of the ray of his glory; the will and image of his hiddenness;[60] [4:5]the all-engendering word of his thought; source of life never-failing from his spring;[61] the all-governing word according to the will of the one who sent it;[62] an image that has no form or likeness among any things that exist. [4:6]This one, by whose power and word all the worlds were set in order and established, is the Son of perfect mercy, is the ray of light of the glory of the Father of ineffable majesty. [4:7]Therefore, know that when this light from that majesty that has no end shines forth for you and will appear like a star to you so that you are able to see him: eagerly, with joy and love, and completely, with care, taking with you his own pure gifts,[63] which were put in the Cave of Treasures of Hidden Mysteries on the Mountain of Victories by your fathers, go to where his light, the star, leads you. [4:8]And you will see a great and amazing sign, God appearing in the bodily form of a human being, unsightly,[64] poor, imperfect, frail, lowly, even the sign of the cross appearing upon him [see *Speculum Humanae Salvationis* on pages 40 and 41]. And you will go before

39

An illuminated manuscript of the *Speculum Humanae Salvationis*, Germany, ca. 1410. The illustrator demonstrates an awareness of the *Revelation of the Magi*, depicting Christ in the form of a star hovering over the Magi. Notice especially the detail of Christ carrying the cross (cf. *Revelation of the Magi* 4:8).

Tres magi viderūt nouā stellā in oriente

Porligāt magnū regn̄ est

him with love and joy, taking with you your gifts, and you will worship in the presence of the child, despised, poor, and killed.[65] [4:9]And you will offer him your gifts, and you shall receive from him the blessing of salvation and shall partake with him in the joy, which, when he comes with his hidden glory, with his perfect divinity, with his perfect riches that do not pass away, with his new world, with his light that [*text missing*], with perfect salvation, which he will give to all [*text missing*]. [4:10]Also, take care and command your sons. And if the coming of the light of the star does not happen in your days, also have your sons tell it to their sons, until the mysteries and revelations shall come to pass that are written about his coming."

5. THE RITUAL OF THE MAGI

[5:1]And we received the laws and commandments from our fathers, and we taught all the mysteries, and we reminded our sons: "Perhaps in your days the coming of the light of this star will happen, as we received and learned from our fathers." [5:2]And we went up to the Mountain of Victories, and when we were all assembled at the foothills of the mountain from each one's dwelling place, we remained in one place for purification on the twenty-fifth day[66] of every month. [5:3]And we bathed in a certain spring that was on the foothills of the mountain, and it is called "The Spring of Purification." [5:4]And seven trees stood over it: an olive, a vine, a myrtle, [a cypress,] an orange, a cedar, and a juniper.[67] [5:5]And that mountain was altogether incomparably more beautiful and desirable than all the mountains in our land, and the smell of all sweet spices effused from it, and the dew that was sprinkled was a sweet smell.[68] [5:6]And when it became the first of the month,[69] we ascended and went to the top of the mountain and stood before the mouth of the Cave of Treasures of Hidden Mysteries. [5:7]And we knelt on our knees and stretched forth our hands to heaven, and we prayed and worshiped in silence, without a sound, to the Father of that heavenly majesty that is ineffable and infinite forever.[70] [5:8]On the third of the month we entered the cave up to the treasures, the treasures that were prepared as the star's own [gifts] and for the adoration of that light that we awaited. [5:9]And what we read and heard from the revelation, when we returned, descending in joy, we said to and instructed our sons, our families, and everyone who gave themselves with love to learn. [5:10]And if it should chance that one of us should pass away, we would raise up his son or one of the sons of his family [in his place,] as when we succeeded our fathers, until the time of the coming of the star has been fulfilled. [5:11]We also taught the people of that country,

43

those who gave themselves to the love of revelation to learn with joy. And those who did not wish to learn and distanced themselves from help because they saw our quiet way of life, that we prayed in silence, [we] said our mysteries to them with honor.[71]

6. **AN EXCERPT FROM SETH'S BOOKS OF REVELATION**

[6:1]Again,[72] from the books that were in the Cave of Treasures of Hidden Mysteries: every word that our father Adam, the beginning of our great lineage, spoke with his son Seth, whom he had after the death of Abel, whom his brother Cain killed[73] and over whom his father Adam mourned. [6:2]And Adam instructed Seth his son about [*text missing*], [and about the revelation] of the light of the star and about its glory, because he [saw] it in the Garden of Eden when it descended and came to rest over the Tree of Life; and it illuminated the entire (garden) before Adam transgressed against the commandment of the Father of heavenly majesty. [6:3]And when he transgressed against the commandment that (the Father) ordained for him, the sight[74] of the star was taken away from him, and (it was also taken away from him) because of his expulsion from Paradise. And Adam our father mourned over (his) foolishness, that he was humbled from his greatness. [6:4]And he strongly warned his son

Seth, and he taught him to walk in righteousness so that he might find mercy before the Father of majesty.

7. THE FALL OF ADAM

^{7:1}And he said to him: "My son, there will be generations and ages from me and from my offspring, and they will be recounting my foolishness and speaking figuratively with figures of speech to one another. ^{7:2}They are fulfilled about me, and they will say: 'Every kingdom that will be divided against itself shall not stand.'[75] This is fulfilled about me, because I doubted about my kingdom in which I stood, and I, by my hands, destroyed it myself. ^{7:3}My son, the rib that was removed from me[76] became a thorn, and it blinded my eye. ^{7:4}I even prophesied when I saw her, and I said: 'This time is bone and flesh from me.'[77] And rightly did I call her 'time,' because she became a stumbling block for me.[78] ^{7:5}My son, guard from her the words of your mouth and do not reveal to her all the mysteries of your heart.[79] ^{7:6}For my compassionate master made her a helper for me,[80] for honor and glory, because he loved me like a beloved son.[81] ^{7:7}And I made her an injury for me and a destroyer of my footprints so that she cast me out of Paradise, my kingdom. ^{7:8}And I did not understand my honor, but I was puffed up in my heart by the advice of treachery that she gave to me, a cup of sound filled with poison by the lie of the serpent.

8. Adam's Ignorance of God's Mercy

46

8:1"And I did not understand my priority when I did not (yet) exist, and when I did exist, in what sort of honor I was, nor my authority over the entire world, nor my love among the holy watchers,[82] nor my entire life inside Paradise, nor, more than everything, the mercy and kindness of my holy master who loved me and was merciful to me like a kind father. 8:2And when I transgressed against his commandment in my boldness, he did not judge me as a Lord who holds a grudge, but as a kind father whose mercy is mixed with discipline. 8:3For if he had judged me according to my foolishness, he would have destroyed me as vanity and made me as if I never existed. And who would stand up against him and say: 'What are you doing?'[83] 8:4But he disciplined me with mercy and did not judge me according to my foolishness, since, behold, my son, I saw the entire creation, which is under my authority as before. 8:5And my deceiver, the Evil One, wanted to humiliate me with his fraud and be liberated from under my authority. On the contrary, my kind master, in his mercy, put him under my feet that I would trample him,[84] having put fear upon me so that I would not obey his advice again. 8:6And like a judge (in) his justice, he shut his lying mouth and filled it with dust, and he tore off his feet so that he could not walk upon them, (and) he

separated him from every animal created like him.[85]
[8:7]And all these things happened to me, my son, and I
was brought low from my majesty. The cause of all these
evil things, Eve your mother, was a stumbling block for
me. [8:8]But you, my son, guard yourself from her advice
and do not obey her as I (did,) but love and honor the
Lord of life, my kind master, and he will save you and
have mercy upon you.

47

9. ADAM'S PREDICTION OF THE END TIMES

[9:1]"For there will be from my family and my children
glorious and honorable people, (the reciters) of the mysteries of the majesty. And they will find great mercy and
will pray, ask, and be heard. [9:2]And [*text missing*] of the
majesty, but at the end times of that generation they will
again be [rebelling,] and they will not be afraid of my
foolishness and of the judgment that I have.[86] Instead,
they shall be headstrong and shall speak blasphemy
unto the heavenly majesty. [9:3]And they will say many
things,[87] and shall also make painted idols and graven
images, and shall even serve the sun and the moon,[88] and
they shall speak words of blasphemy. [9:4]And all these
things that are among them from the deceits of my
treacherous deceiver, because he will offer the love of his
fraud and his deceit filled with poison to each of the generations that will be after me. [9:5]And he will [show] and

make them desire the empty praise of great riches, pride, clothes, property, fornication, boastfulness, injustice, greed, and various possessions. ⁹ᐟ⁶And he will appear to them like a lover or a friend and entice them. And again, with reveling, drunkenness, impure and defiled feasts, which are an illusion [of his] empty [apparitions,] and again, with possessions of assorted excesses, he will take hold of them with fraudulent affection, which is not virtuous,⁸⁹ just as also to me through Eve.

48

10. ADAM'S FINAL EXHORTATION TO SETH

¹⁰ᐟ¹"He led me astray by his fraudulent word like an innocent person concerned for my welfare: 'See, I promise you something right and suitable for you, (namely) that, when you have eaten from the tree, from which you were commanded not to eat, you will become like your God,'⁹⁰ my merciful master. ¹⁰ᐟ²I, wretch (that I was), did not understand my honor, that his fraudulent promise could not come true, nor could the clay be like its potter,⁹¹ nor the servant like his master.⁹² But I know the great mercy of the majesty of my kind master, which is to be revealed for me at the end of days. ¹⁰ᐟ³And at the end he will save me from destruction and raise me from the dust as he raised me up when I did not exist.⁹³ And my enemy rejoiced and exulted over me since I had fallen by his deceit. ¹⁰ᐟ⁴My kind savior and merciful master is going to

sustain me and have pity upon me with his mercy, and [descending] to the darkness,[94] he will strengthen me by his light and illuminate my eyes as he did before, (when) he breathed the spirit into my nostrils and I lived.[95] [10:5]But you, my son, and your generations after you, it has pleased my maker and my savior that you should find mercy before him; for he does not reckon against you my own sins because of his kindness. [10:6]For if he had requited me according to my foolishness, I would not have begotten forth fruits,[96] nor would he have accepted the offering from your brother Abel,[97] nor would he have exacted retribution for his blood from the hands of his brother who killed him.[98] [10:7]For he does not neglect in his great mercy anyone who loves him and walks in justice before him. Even to those who offend him, he gives opportunity for repentance, and is gracious to them if they repent and seek (it) from him, because his mercy upon his world is great." [10:8]And Seth heard everything that his father Adam commanded him, commandments more numerous than these, and wrote them down with diligence, and we found them in the books that were placed in the Cave of Treasures of Hidden Mysteries. [10:9]He also commanded and added to them. And Seth purified his heart so that he would not obey the deceitful Evil One, and he praised and called upon the name of the Father of heavenly majesty.[99] [10:10]And Seth also commanded these mysteries to his sons. And we were reading (them) every

49

month that we went up the mountain, and with love we entered the Cave of Treasures of Hidden Mysteries. And we also learned them and taught our sons and families.

11. THE APPEARANCE OF THE STAR TO THE MAGI

[11:1]Then, when the time and fulfillment of what was written in the books happened, concerning the revelation of the light of the hidden star, we were indeed thought worthy for it to come in our days and to receive it with joy, as we were commanded by our fathers and as we ourselves read in the books. [11:2]And each of us saw wondrous and diverse visions that were never before seen by us, but their mysteries were in these books that we were reading.[100] [11:3]And each one came from his dwelling place according to our ancient custom to ascend the Mountain of Victories [*text missing*] to wash in the Spring of Purification, as we were accustomed. [11:4]And we saw [*text missing*] in the form of an ineffable pillar of light descending, and it came to rest above the water. [11:5]And we were afraid and shook when we saw it. And we cannot speak about the brilliance of the star of light, since its radiance was many times greater than the sun, and the sun could not stand out before the light of its rays.[101] [11:6]And just like the moon looks in the daytime in the days of Nisan,[102] when the sun rises and it is absorbed in its light,[103] so also

Panel of polyptych from the workshop of Rogier van
der Weyden, mid-fifteenth century, the Cloisters
Collection, New York. A similar work to the
frontispiece of this book, this painting depicts several
details from the *Revelation of the Magi*. Note the infant
Christ in the form of a star, the holy mountain of the
Magi, and the Magi bathing in their sacred spring.

did the sun seem to us when the star rose over us. [11:7]And the light of the star, which surpassed the sun, appeared to us ourselves and the sons of our mysteries,[104] but it did not appear to anyone else,[105] because they were removed from its mysteries and its coming. And we rejoiced, and glorified, and gave unmeasured thanks to the Father of heavenly majesty that it appeared in our days and we were thought worthy to see it.

52

12. THE STAR DESCENDS TO THE MOUNTAIN OF VICTORIES

[12:1]And when we bathed in the Spring of Purification with joy, and we ascended the Mountain of Victories as we were accustomed, and we went up and found that pillar of light in front of the cave, again a great fear came upon us [see detail of polyptych by Rogier van der Weyden on page 51]. [12:2]And [we knelt] upon our knees, and we stretched out our hands according to our ancient custom, and we praised in silence the vision of its wonders. [12:3]And again, we saw that heaven had been opened[106] like a great gate and men of glory carrying the star of light upon their hands. And they descended and stood upon the pillar of light,[107] and the entire mountain was filled by its light, which cannot be uttered by the mouth of humanity. [12:4]And (something) like the hand of a small person drew near in our eyes from the pillar and the star, at which we could not look, and it comforted us. And we saw the star enter the Cave of Treasures of Hidden Mysteries, and the cave shone beyond measure.[108] 12:5And a humble and kind voice made itself heard by us, which called out and said to us: "Enter inside without doubt, in love, and see a great and amazing vision." And we were encouraged and comforted by the message of the voice. 12:6And we entered, being afraid, and we bowed our knees at the mouth of the cave because of the very abundance of the light. 12:7And when we rose at its command, we lifted our eyes and saw that light, which is unspeakable by the mouth of human beings.

13. EPIPHANY IN THE CAVE OF TREASURES

13:1And when it had concentrated itself, it appeared to us in the bodily form of a small and humble human,[109] and he said to us: "Peace to you,[110] sons of my hidden mysteries."[111] And again, we were astonished by the vision, and he said to us: "Do not doubt the vision that you have seen, that there has appeared to you that ineffable light of the voice of the hidden Father of heavenly majesty. 13:2And again, (do not doubt that) it appeared to you to concentrate its light in its rays, or that it appeared to you in the form of a small, humble, and unworthy human, because indeed, the inhabitants of the world cannot bear to see the glory of the only Son of the Father of majesty,[112] unless it appeared for them in the form of their world. [13:3]And again, other signs shall appear in it, which are hidden and (would be) shameful for the heavenly majesty, for the sake of the redemption of the lives of human beings, because my Father has loved them that they should not perish[113] by the error in which they have persisted. [13:4]And again, I will perfect[114] the love of the Father, even unto the death of a cross.[115] For the sake of their salvation I will descend to raise them up with me in love and indivisible peace if they shall believe in me without doubt, and give thanks, and glorify through me the Father of that glorious majesty who sent me for their salvation. [13:5]And I have loved them that they may not perish by the error in which they have persisted. And therefore, since I have appeared to them in the fullness of all the times,[116] they have no excuse[117] for their offenses unless they repent and believe in me. [13:6]And also you, everything that you were commanded by your fathers, and everything that you learned from the mysteries of the books that you have read, do, since behold, the hidden mysteries of the light of the star that you have been waiting to see, behold, he himself has (now) told you about himself as you are able to hear. [13:7]And you will believe without doubt, seeing in me signs of many forms. [13:8]And again, take with you the treasure that was deposited in this cave by your fathers and [continue in joy] and worship the [*text missing*] I will be born like a human being. ¹³:⁹And again, worship me there [*text missing*]: even now, as I am speaking with you I am also there. Because my Gospel has been proclaimed by angels, I am both there and with the majesty of my Father.[118] ¹³:¹⁰And I am everywhere,[119] because I am a ray of light whose light has shone in this world from the majesty of my Father, who has sent me to fulfill everything that was spoken about me in the entire world and in every land by unspeakable mysteries,[120] and to accomplish the commandment of my glorious Father, who by the prophets preached about me to the contentious house,[121] in the same way as for you, as befits your faith, it was revealed to you about me.[122] ¹³:¹¹And I am going up with you and am a guide for you on the entire journey that you are traveling, seeing signs, glorious wonders, and great victories upon the entire earth. And you will see the completion of all the mysteries in Jerusalem, and everything that was spoken with you will come true for you. ¹³:¹²And again, you will see signs of humility, even a lowly and weak form, such that people will act boldly against me, and they will desire to do that which they plotted in deceit against me, and they will not be able to have [their goal] take place. ¹³:¹³But all that they do will be for their killing and their destruction,[123]

55

and the will of the Father shall be fulfilled for the sake of the salvation of the life of the whole world."

14. THE MAGI REALIZE CHRIST'S POLYMORPHISM

[14:1]And when he spoke all these things with us, along with a great many that we cannot say because of the great riches of their majesty, all of us went out of the cave, exulting and rejoicing that we were thought worthy for all these mysteries of that unspeakable majesty to be revealed around us and spoken with us. [14:2]And we took that entire treasure that was deposited in the cave, letters having been sealed in which it was placed.[124] And we descended from the mountain, glorifying the mysteries of the revelations of the light of the star that appeared to us. [14:3]And each of us was speaking about the revelations and visions that had appeared to him in the Cave of Treasures of Hidden Mysteries, but our visions did not resemble each other, and all the wonders of many forms that appeared to us.[125] [14:4]"There is one of us saying, "I saw a light in which there were many images that were amazing." And there is one saying, "I saw an infant who had unspeakable forms." [14:5]And there is one saying, "I saw a youth who did not have a form in this world." And there is one saying, "I saw a human being who was humble, unsightly in appearance,[126] and poor." [14:6]And there is one saying, "I saw a cross and a person of light who hung upon it, taking away the sins of the entire world."[127] And there is one saying, "I saw that he went down to Sheol with force and all the dead rose and worshiped him."[128] [14:7]And there is one saying, "I saw that he ascended in glory, and he opened the graves, and he raised up the dead, while they are crying out and saying: 'Holy is our king and holy is his descent to us! Because of our sins he humbled himself to save us.'" [14:8]And there is one saying, "I saw him ascending to the heavenly height, and angels opening the gates[129] of heaven before him. And clouds of seraphs and angels are taking him upon the palms of their hands,[130] and the Paraclete Spirit[131] taking a diadem and a crown and making victory shine before him, and all the hosts praising and singing the honor of his humility, which prevailed in the whole struggle of error and death." [14:9]And when all these things and others like them, of which there were many, (happened,) while descending the Mountain of Victories, we gave praise and repeated to each other everything that we saw and heard there. [14:10]And we were in great rejoicing and great exultation that we were thought worthy to see this complete gift of salvation for which all the kings, and righteous ones, and prophets, and powerful ones prayed, and hoped, and waited, that they might see this sight. But they did not see it[132] because it was not then the time of the coming of the star of light, giving perfect salvation to its believers.

15. THE FATHER SPEAKS TO THE MAGI

[15:1]And while we were praising these things, suddenly a voice with much light[133] and with unspeakable kindness came to our ears from the heavenly height of majesty, saying to us: "Everything that you have seen, and heard, and discussed, and had spoken to you, and (at which) behold, you are amazed, is (only) one drop of salvation from the house of [majesty.] [15:2]For there is no one who can know all the mysteries of singleness except the one who is issued from the thought of the hiddenness of the Father. And no one knows the Father except[134] the voice bringing forth the word of salvation, revealing the depth of hiddenness of the thought of the Father, in whom he is forever.[135] [15:3]And by the (same) voice and word the heavenly worlds and the lower ones of the Father of majesty came into being and were ordered:[136] the angels, and powers, and princes, and authorities, even this world in which you exist, and the height, and depth, and length, and width.[137] [15:4]And there is otherwise nothing that exists outside the will of the Father of majesty[138] or that has come to be without the voice of life. For this is my beloved Son,[139] being sent of perfect love. This is the revealer of the secrets of the Father for his beloved ones, as it is fitting for them and as they can receive by his gift[140] of the Son. [15:5]This is he who has told of new and perfect worlds for those who are persuaded and believe in him. This is the interpreter of wisdom and hidden mysteries. This is he who is the image and form of the Father of majesty,[141] by whom he is always heard. [15:6]This is the only begotten Son,[142] perfecting all the will of his Father. This is the one who is not loved and honored as he deserves, because that world loves the darkness and its desires more than him.[143] [15:7]This is the one who was humbled and became a human being for the salvation of human beings so that they would not perish. He put on, by his will, a body,[144] a humble form, that with it he might slay death and take away the dominion of death, to give eternal life to those who love him and believe in him. [15:8]This is the one in whose name signs and portents take place through his believers.[145] This is the perfect Son, doing the will of he who sent him. This one is the way[146] and the gate[147] of light for those who enter by it. [15:9]This is the one who is in everything and is named and spoken of above all.[148] This is the bread of life that comes down from me[149] for believers; he is the sower of the word of life,[150] and he is the shepherd of truth who gives himself as ransom for his flock.[151] He is the great priest[152] who by his blood absolves the worlds; he is a drink[153] of the vine[154] of life. [15:10]This is the one that you saw who is in many forms that appeared to you, but is not deprived of either my love or the person of his glory. And no one exists over him or over his majesty to speak of how he is, except me, and I and he, we are one in unspeakable glory."

16. THE MIRACULOUS JOURNEY

[16:1]And when all these things and many others were spoken about the revelation that appeared to us, the star was with us in all (its) excellent forms so we could see it. And we spoke about it like frail human beings, not being able to say anything that we saw. [16:2]And we got ready with our whole encampment,[155] and with our provisions, and with the pure and holy gifts, those that we brought out of the Cave of Treasures of Hidden Mysteries, in which they were [deposited] previously by our fathers, and we went forth in great joy, our hearts exulting to come to the place that was commanded to us, to worship the vision of the star of infinite light. [16:3]And the star, our guide, our good messenger, our perfect light, our glorious leader, again appeared for us, going before us and upholding[156] our whole caravan from all sides, and enlightening us by its hidden light. [see *The Journey of the Magi* on pages 62 and 63]. [16:4]And we had no need of the light of the sun or of the moon,[157] because their light became diminished in its sight, and by night and by day we walked in its light, exulting and rejoicing without distress or weariness.[158] [16:5]And it prepared before us a blessed dwelling place in which to reside while we rested and exulted. Even our provisions were abundant in our eyes and did not decrease, but rather from one day to another they increased when it[159] came to rest over us with its light.[160] 16:6And it gave rest to us from all our fatigue as if we were not journeying on the road, and it made mountains, and hills, and rugged places level before us.[161] Even the rivers before us we crossed by foot without fear, because of the light of our good guide that went along with us for our encampment. And again, when we crossed into the places [of beasts and vicious snakes,] we trampled them with our feet.[162] 16:7And our leader and our guide, in his glory, appeared to each one of us in all forms and appearances in every (stage). And he filled our hearts with great joy, and all the (stages) in which we journeyed were short and swift in our eyes, because our victorious sign and our powerful light, which is beyond every human mouth to speak, guided us with its victorious strength.

61

17. THE MAGI IN JERUSALEM

17:1And when we arrived in the region of Jerusalem, in the month of flowers,[163] our good emissary led and brought us inside Jerusalem. 17:2And its nobles and rulers were disturbed and troubled,[164] and they asked us: "On account of what cause have you come here? Perhaps because of the mysteries of your Magianism?" because they saw us looking up at heaven, and worshiping our sign, and praying to our guide, because they did not understand our mysteries, and they reckoned us as Magi.[165]

The Journey of the Magi by Sassetta, Metropolitan Museum of Art, New York, ca. 1435. Similar to the description found in chapter 16 of the *Revelation of the Magi,* this painting depicts the Star of Bethlehem as being in close proximity to the traveling Magi.

[17:3]And we said to them: "We saw a sign of heavenly majesty in our land, as we were instructed by our fathers, that a king, and a messiah, and a life giver, and a savior who gives himself to death for the sake of the entire world has been born here. [17:4]And we have come because we saw all his signs and the forms of his hidden divinity in the appearance of a human clothed with a body.[166] And we came, rejoicing with our pure gifts, which were deposited by our fathers in the Cave of Treasures of Hidden Mysteries on the Mountain of Victories. [17:5]And he commanded us in a great vision to come to this land to worship him in reverence, because he has worshipers in every country.[167] He becomes for them a life giver, and a savior, and a forgiver of sins, and through him the Lord of all is pleased with his creation and makes atonement with his people." [17:6]And Herod, the governor of the region, called and sent for the honorable elders of the city, and asked them: "Where is it written that the king messiah, and savior, and life giver of the worlds is to be born?"[168] And all of them said to him (as) from one mouth: "The village Bethlehem, as was said by the heavenly majesty to our father David, the ancient prophet who lived a long time ago." [17:7]And when we heard from them what they said, again we rejoiced greatly. And while we were exulting, we saw our leader and our guide; again we abounded in joy all the more.[169] [17:8]And while we spoke mysteries, and all manner of revelations, and praises, we went in joy to Bethlehem as the blind scribes had read, not believing what they read from their books,[170] nor Herod, the blind governor, [unseeing] of the love of the light that was born in their land, which (was) the light before (all) worlds.[171] And they are dwelling in darkness in the world in their days.[172] [17:9]But Herod said to us in his deceit: "When you have seen the messiah, come and tell me, that I also may go to worship him."[173] And because he was not worthy for the worship of the light that was born, because he was a dwelling of error, it was said to us by our guide and our light that we should not return to him,[174] because he was not [worthy] to see the great light of the world,[175] because he was totally deaf and blind to its worship.

65

18. ARRIVAL IN BETHLEHEM

[18:1]And we went and entered Bethlehem in joy, which was worthy to be called the village for the holy birth and for the great light that appeared in it (to kill) and destroy all error and to bring death to an end. [18:2]And all of us went to the homestead[176] in which our guide was born, and we saw a cave[177] like the form and appearance of the Cave of Treasures of Hidden Mysteries,[178] which is in our country, from which we had learned the hidden mysteries that were preached about him, which were deposited in it by our ancient fathers, and they were all accomplished today in our coming here.[179] [18:3]And we saw the pillar of light, which descended as we had seen it before,[180] and it stood in front of the cave, and that star of light descended and stood above the pillar, angels on its right side and on its left side.[181] [18:4]And when we saw it, again we rejoiced, though being afraid. And the pillar, and the star, and the angels entered and went before us into that cave,[182] in which the mystery and light of salvation was born. [18:5]And a compassionate voice instructed us, "Enter inside,"[183] and we went in after it, and we took our crowns,[184] and we put them under his feet, because the everlasting kingdom is his.[185] [18:6]And we knelt and worshiped before him upon the earth, because every knee that is in heaven and on earth bows to him and worships him.[186] [18:7]And we opened our hidden treasures, and they being sealed, we took them and came near the treasure of salvation, who is sealed with heavenly majesty. [18:8]And we brought forth our treasures before him, who is the treasure of salvation, that we might receive them from him in the kingdom by many-fold before his own judgment seat of salvation.[187]

66

19. Epiphany in the Bethlehem Cave

[19:1]And the glorious infant and the ancient light perfecting the will of the Father of majesty opened his mouth, and he said to us with a love of abundant and sweet mercy: "Peace to you, sons of my hidden mysteries,[188] sons of the East, of the heavenly light, because you have been found worthy to see the ancient everlasting light, you and also your fathers.[189] [19:2]And as you were worthy, behold, you have received him in perfect love without doubt. And again, you will be worthy to see him in his great light before which there will no longer be any mysteries, because they all are fulfilled in him. [19:3]And he alone from this time onward rules over all, and all are subject to him. [19:4]For it was I who was revealed to you in your land, and I spoke with you by mysteries. And again, I became for you a guide and leader to this place until you came in peace before me. [19:5]And again, I shall be with you even until the end,[190] and I am not separated from you nor from all those who believe in me with perfect love. [19:6]And again, you will be witnesses for me in the land of the East together with my disciples,[191] those who are chosen by me to preach my Gospel. [19:7]And when I have completed the will of my Father regarding everything that he commanded me, (I will go up) in the glory in which I was with him.[192] Yet even now, while I am speaking with you, I am with him and have not become separated from the majesty of the Father.[193] [19:8]Now I shall give to you another sign at which you will be astonished: in the hour that you see the sun darkened in the daytime like the night,[194] and there is a great earthquake upon the earth, and the voice of the dead is heard from their graves giving praise,[195] then at that time know that all the times and seasons have come to an end in my coming to you. [19:9]And lift your eyes to the (heavens), and see them opened in glory before me, and I am ascending in praise fitting for me and sitting at the right hand of the Father of majesty,[196] from whom I have been sent to save the world."

68

20. ANGELS PRAISE CHRIST

[20:1]And while the savior was speaking all these things with us, that entire cave shone,[197] and it became in our eyes like another world, since [in this world] there was no light like it. [20:2]And many voices of [seraphs] were speaking and [*text missing*] which are innumerable: "Yea and Amen![198] [20:3]O first-born opener of the secret womb, O holy infant, O completer of the will of the heavenly majesty who is the perfect 'Yes,' and through whom everything came into being,[199] and 'Amen,'[200] by your light and by your word they were made perfect, and all the worlds seen and unseen were brought to completion.[201] [20:4]And all the angels and the powers worship you. And yours is the place of salvation, which you will give to your chosen ones. And yours is the ancient light, because you are the beloved fruit of the thought of the Father. [20:5]And you are the image and will of the one who upholds all, the revealer of hidden things, because by the word that is spoken all that is in the thought is made known. And you are all, and all is in you, and there is nothing outside of your will."[202]

21. THE COMMISSIONING OF THE MAGI

[21:1]And when all these praises were spoken and we heard, we were afraid and trembled, and we fell upon the ground like dead men. [21:2]And the child, the offspring of light, stretched out his right hand mightily and put it upon us.[203] And he comforted us and said to us: "Sons of my mysteries,[204] do not be afraid. For all these things that you have seen and heard from the first day until today, and at which you are amazed: even those ones that [you hear] are not greater than I am, but for you they are mighty because you are clothed in weak flesh, yet for me they are very small things. [21:3]For because of your frailty, you are not able to see or hear a single one of the wonderful things that belong to me with the Father who sent me. But since you have been found worthy to see and hear these things at this time—and behold, you are amazed as wonderful things are in your sight!—again you shall be deemed worthy by my love, which is with you forever, to see and hear these great things that cannot be spoken now. And neither watchers nor angels are able to speak of them, because these things are very great even for them.[205] [21:4]Therefore, rise and go in peace to your light-receiving land,[206] because you have been deemed worthy to receive the perfect light of the heavenly majesty, and to come and worship it with your gifts in joy. Behold, you have completed everything that you were commanded by your fathers, and you have also been deemed worthy to know and learn the ancient hidden mysteries, which were written for you from the first generations. Now, behold, you have seen the completion of your mysteries, and you have completed everything that you have been commanded for my love and for my witness. [21:5]And again, you have been deemed worthy to be witnesses for me in the East with my disciples, who were chosen by me before the world came to be. And when I have completed the will of my Father regarding everything that he commanded me and have ascended to him in glory, I shall send to you some of my chosen ones who have been chosen by me for your land. And they shall speak and witness the truth with you that it may be your seal[207] with one accord. [21:6]Therefore, rise and go in peace. Again, I am with you in all visions and signs,[208] just as I am with you from the first day. For just as I am in sight and in all forms here—and behold, you are amazed by all the visions and forms in which you see me—I am also with the Father of majesty whose will I am since the world began, and I am never separated from you, nor from the presence of the Father, because I am a ray of his light, and I was sent to you to enlighten you. [21:7]And behold, you are amazed as frail human beings—how much more

70

when I have come to you in the majesty of my Father. As for you not being able to stand before me, neither (could) the angels and powers that are above you when I descended upon them, and they saw a vision of wonders and stood in fear and trembling. Even as it was fitting for them I appeared to them, and for you I appeared as you were able to see. [21:8]For the Father of majesty does not have an image and form in this world,[209] except I who am an epiphany from him, since I am his will, and his power, and his wisdom,[210] since I am in my Father and my Father is in me.[211] And I am—as it is fitting for God to be seen and for the world to know him, and again, as the sons of wisdom can receive and hear with love—the majesty of the Father who sent me. And now I have appeared to you in the form of humanity to fulfill everything that is written about me.[212] [21:9]Because of the reason and the foolishness of your ancient father Adam's sin, which became your downfall to Sheol, death has had authority over you, and error has reigned in deceit over your generations and has supposed in its rashness that it was lord over you and that you had become its property forever. And again, I have made known to you, your fathers, and even to that ancient race of yours, your freedom, because you are from the race of light.[213] And it was not in vain that you were created in the world, and heaven, and earth, and all the worlds came into being for your sake.[214] [21:10]And also, the Father of majesty, because

71

of this love, sent me, and I clothed myself in your form, that by it I might bring to an end and destroy all those who afflict you and your captors. And I shall offer you to the Father, before him as a pure and perfect offering, since there are no blemishes of error on you. And I shall set you free with love, and with truth, with pure water, and the birth of the Holy Spirit,[215] and you shall be for me by love brothers and believers, like infants in whom there are no blemishes of evil,[216] from now until forever. [21:11]Therefore, joy, and praise, and thanksgiving he[217] will cause to go up from you in the heavenly heights from you through me, since I am his will. And joy, and redemption, and the fellowship of the Spirit, and eternal life shall be given to you through me, since everything is in agreement without division. As from the beginning under the wings[218] of the Father will it be, his power, and his wisdom, and his righteous will sanctifying and having mercy upon you forever and ever." [21:12]And again, a voice from on high, and from every direction, and from inside the earth was heard, which answered and said, "Amen! The will of complete salvation, joy and peace to all the worlds!"[219]

22. THE MAGI MEET MARY AND JOSEPH

[22:1]And when we received from him the commandments of salvation, we went forth from his presence in great joy, and much exultation, and with praise, our hearts being filled with great hope, to come to our land. [22:2]And Joseph and Mary, honored and blessed people, went out with us,[220] they who were deemed worthy and entrusted to be called by the name parents and to be upbringers for the offspring of the voice of virgin hearing[221] and upbringers for the perfect will of complete mercy. Mary became the gate for the great light that entered the world in grace to banish the darkness. [22:3]And she became the way of salvation for God giving birth to himself,[222] who appeared in the bodily form of a human being.[223] And there will be for her a name, and a memory, and a blessing forever and ever.[224] [22:4]And they lifted up their eyes and they saw the light that was born by his mercy in their house,[225] which is with us and accompanies us. [22:5]And they said to us: "We were not pleased by your coming to us. You have led away the light and the great hope of the whole world, and you have gone away [with him] and [have deprived us] of him. We were deemed worthy by great grace to be trusted to be attendants for it, for the upbringing of the body that appeared in our house,[226] and now, behold, we have seen him going away with you."

73

23. THE MAGI'S REVELATION TO MARY

[23:1]We said to her: "O woman blessed among women,[227] O blessed Mary, who was deemed worthy by mercy to

receive the conception of the Spirit by your pure obedience and to bring forth the child of salvation of the eternal word, you were trusted and deemed worthy to be
called mother for him. ²³:²And now, behold, your glorious
child is inside of you,²²⁸ and behold, he awaits you in the
house, even while he is not separated from us, as he said
to us, because he is the great gift of salvation that by
your child was given to all the worlds. ²³:³And the mystery that was hidden from the beginning in the Father of
all has been revealed to us in your child. And the treasure of salvation has appeared which had been kept for
all generations. This great gift and light of salvation is
not yours alone, but is (for) all the heavenly and lower
worlds. ²³:⁴And lift up your eyes and see that he is in the
entire creation and enlightens it all, and it is full of his
glorious mysteries. And now he has appeared in the
world in a body, and the forms with him are seen in
every land, because he has been sent by his²²⁹ majesty for
the salvation and redemption of every human being."²³⁰

24. (M)ARY SPEAKS TO CHRIST

²⁴:¹And when Joseph and Mary turned back, rejoicing
about all these things that they had heard about the holy
child, they went away to their house.²³¹ ²⁴:²And Mary entered and found the child of light laughing²³² about and
glorifying all his great and amazing mysteries, pro-

claimed in the entire world from [ancient times,] and behold, all of them are fulfilled in his appearance today. And he glorified and gave thanks to his Father who sent him for the redemption of his worlds. [24:5]And Mary and Joseph worshiped him, and she said to him: "I have rejoiced that I have seen the treasury of salvation, and my light, and the holy child, who is the obedience of my ears.[233] [24:4]And O opener of my womb by [your] holy mercy, O Lord of my holy virginity, I have greatly rejoiced that I have found my great treasure in my house where I gave birth and my great light, which exists forever. I had thought, O my beloved, that the Easterners were taking you, with your great love for them, in exchange for the gifts they offered to you from your own, since I saw your holy form going along with them."[234]

75

25. CHRIST BLESSES MARY

[25:1]And he answered in a sweet and humble voice and said to Mary: "Peace to you,[235] my mother and upbringer, since you were deemed worthy to be blessed among women,[236] since you were deemed worthy for the fruit of the voice of salvation. Since you accepted and conceived with love in your mind and with faith without doubt, you shall receive the reward of your service and shall have blessing and remembrance in all (the) generations,[237] and in the new world you shall receive a good reward.

^{25:2}And because of you, Eve and her offspring will have hope and salvation, since by your person you have made her pass beyond the spear that fenced in the Tree of Life.[238] ^{25:3}And by your person tranquillity and peace have happened for all the worlds from now on and forever, Amen! For I, who appeared in your house, have come to fulfill the will of the Father who sent me, and everyone who hears me and believes shall live. For behold, you have perfectly accomplished your own service without a flaw, for which you shall receive a good recompense. ^{25:4}Therefore, I am turning to all my brethren who are in the entire world, that I may perfectly fulfill everything that the Father commanded me for my believers, so that they may bring forth the fruits of eternal salvation. And I shall also give to them all the promises of my Father, which through me are fulfilled, and are given, and are accomplished for my believers and everyone who believes in me."

26. THE RETURN JOURNEY HOME

^{26:1}And when we came to the first (stage), again the sign of light appeared to us in front of us, and we rejoiced and exulted greatly, and we knelt and worshiped upon the ground before it. ^{26:2}And we glorified the vision, and we answered in our voice as one and said to it: "We worship and give thanks for your kindness and your light, which

accompanies [our] encampment everywhere." [26:3]And he answered and said to us: "I am everywhere,[239] and there is no land in which I am not. I am also where you departed from me, for I am greater than the sun, and there is no place in the world that is deprived of it, even though it[240] is a single entity; yet if it departs from the world, all its inhabitants sit in darkness. How much more I, who am the Lord of the sun, and my light and word are more abundant [by many times] than the sun." [26:4]And we answered and said before him: "O our light and our savior, we know all these things, and they are true for us. And we believe that all these wonders that we saw with all your believers[241] are, for your majesty, small things. But for us they are powerful, and no mouth can speak of them or acknowledge any of them." [26:5]And when the time of supper came, we brought out some of our provisions to refresh ourselves, and we saw that our provisions were replenished beyond those provisions that came out of our country with us when we came.[242] And then, again, we were all the more afraid, glorifying the majesty that was with us, which did not hold back from our weakness. [26:6]And when we ate our supper from the food in passing the night, each of us spoke joy and praise. As with a fountain that spouts forth much water, so the visions and wonders did not resemble each other.[243] [26:7]And we spoke to and glorified our guide, and our leader, and the light of our encampment, and the many

77

forms, and his glorious vestments, and his beautiful images, and his perfect likenesses, which were with us.

27. THE MAGI ADDRESS THE PEOPLE OF SHIR

[27:1]And we journeyed on all (our stages) with his glorious signs until we came to our borders, and all our families, children, and a multitude of the people of our land came out to meet us. [27:2]And when they heard that we had come, they met us with great joy and received us, rejoicing, and exulting, and glorifying. And they marveled at our appearance and the health of our entire encampment.[244] [27:3]And when we went to them, they assembled and came before us. And we began to speak and narrate for them about[245] how our ascent took place, and about the astounding visions that accompanied us, and about our entrance into Jerusalem, and about everything that was spoken with us, and about our journeying to Bethlehem, and about the glorious visions and revelations of the Father of heavenly majesty, which appeared to us in the cave: a great light and wondrous appearances in the bodily form of a humble human being, and about his light of the star, which went before us as a glorious guide. [27:4]And when, again, we entered and saw before us the unspeakable glory, and we fell and worshiped the divine child of great light, two angels were standing by and a pillar of cloud[246] was standing by, like all the visions that we saw previ-

ously on the Mountain of Victories in the Cave of Treasures of Hidden Mysteries, which is in our land. Also, in that cave everything was accomplished in truth, even about the forms and vestments of the glorious and divine child who appeared to us in the cave of Bethlehem.[247]
[27:5]And he spoke to us and taught us, "Behold, all the mysteries, and parables, and forms, and revelations are fulfilled, and everything that has been spoken about me by the prophets and in the whole world from the first day until today.[248] From now on let the will of he who sent me be accomplished in me regarding everything that he sent me to fulfill." [27:6]And we offered him gifts that we took from the Cave of Treasures, which were deposited by our fathers from his own.[249] And we worshiped him, the Lord of worship, and he opened his splendid and glorious mouth and spoke [salvation] with us as we were able and sufficient to hear it,[250] and in this way he planted the word of salvation in us. [27:7]And he spoke and revealed to us concerning the place of salvation and concerning the heavenly kingdom of the Father of majesty, the Lord of all, who sent him for the healing of the worlds, to cure their sickness, because they could not be healed by one of the ancient prophets,[251] but only through the will of the Son of perfect mercy. [27:8]And he dismissed us to come to our land in peace, and when we came to the first stage, rejoicing and exulting the entire way, again we found our guide and our light with all the forms that we saw before us.[252]

79

And we trembled and were greatly afraid, worshiping and glorifying his majesty, which accompanied our encampment. [27:9]And also, our provisions were filling our vessels, overflowing from his blessings, and were even more than the provisions that we had taken with us when we set out to go.[253] And behold, they are sitting filled before your[254] eyes, our vessels overflowing from them, because of the power of his blessings, which settled upon us, and so that they might be proved true for you and you might believe everything—the visions and wonders that we saw—and that you also might be deemed worthy to become believers and chosen ones for him. [27:10]And his great power and his revelations will indeed stay with you, because he is also here [with us] in truth, as he spoke to us,[255] and we believe that his light is not removed from our encampment. Indeed, again, he is in the entire world, for he is the light that is all-sufficient and all-enlightening[256] by his perfect love.[257] [27:11]Everyone who wishes, receive without doubt, with a whole heart and true faith, and eat from these provisions, which have come with us. And be deemed worthy, and you, too, join in his blessing, which accompanies us and is with us forever.

28. THE PEOPLE EAT THE MAGI'S FOOD

[28:1]And some of the people,[258] rejoicing in love, took of those provisions and ate. And they began rejoicing and leaping for joy, while glorifying and saying to each other everything that appeared to them.[259] There was one of them saying, "At the moment I ate of these provisions, I saw a great light that has no likeness in the world." [28:2]And there is one saying, "I saw God bearing himself[260] in the world as he wished." And there is one saying, "I saw a star of light that darkened the sun by its light."[261] And there is one saying, "I saw a human being whose appearance is more unsightly than a man,[262] and he is saving and purifying the world by his blood and by his humble appearance." [28:3]And there is one saying, "I saw something like a lamb[263] hanging upon a tree of life,[264] and by him and his blood redemption takes place for all the creatures of the world." And there is one saying, "I saw a pillar of light diving down inside the bowels of the earth, and the dead rise to meet it, and they worship and glorify it with great joy." [28:4]And those who ate from those provisions were speaking to each other many other things beyond these, and their minds brought forth much glory day by day. And there was great joy in the entire land of the East, and the nobles, and the poor, and women, and children from the entire land were gathered together[265] in the love of our Lord[266] before those nobles who were called Magi.[267] [28:5]And they[268] came and heard from them[269] the new and glorious teaching,[270] and the mysteries, and the revelations, and everything that was spoken with them from that

81

first day that they went out from their land until they came back in joy. And again, day by day, revelations, and visions, and all kinds of powerful manifestations were increased for them. [28:6]And the faith increased with the love of the testimony of our Lord Jesus Christ,[271] by the mighty works which he did through them, that offspring of light who appeared to them until he accomplished the will of the one who sent him in everything and was taken up with glory to that heavenly height, his first abode. And the faith of salvation increased in the land of the East in those who heard.[272]

29. JUDAS THOMAS ARRIVES IN SHIR

[29:1]When, again, Judas Thomas[273] went down there by the will of our Lord when he sent him, again the faith increased all the more in those who heard, through the many mighty works and signs that Judas Thomas, the apostle of our Lord, was doing there. [29:2]And when the nobles had heard that Judas had gone there, as the light that appeared to them had said,[274] they gathered together and went to him to meet with him in prayer and faith. And they saluted Judas with complete love, rejoicing in our Lord. [29:3]And Judas also greatly rejoiced with them, and while they were with him for (several) days,[275] they related to Judas how they were deemed worthy to receive from the first day this gift of the light of the world, and about[276] their ascent to him at Bethlehem and everything that was spoken with them, and about the revelations and visions that they saw there in the cave, and about their descent, how he, in his light, accompanied their entire encampment with many visions and revelations. [29:4]And when Judas the Apostle recognized that the gift of our Lord had overflowed upon them, he also related to them about our savior while all the brethren were gathered together as one, and about the mighty works, and healings, and wonders, which he did in the very sight of his apostles, and about the forms of his images, and about his astounding appearances, about which we are not able to narrate, since he was always appearing to us so that we were amazed[277] by him, and we stood in the outpouring and in the doubt of mind,[278] since no one had ever appeared in such a way in the days of the world. [29:5]And when all the brethren heard what Judas related to them, they all glorified with one voice the Lord of heavenly majesty through his Son, the will of perfect salvation. And they sought from Judas, the apostle of our Lord, to make them partakers with him in the seal[279] of our Lord. [29:6]And Judas said: "My brothers, I also rejoice, because it is for this gift that I was sent in salvation, since everyone who believes in salvation and with love receives the seal of my Lord Jesus Christ in truth, the Enemy does not rule over."

83

30. THE HYMN OF JUDAS THOMAS

30:1Then at night, before Sunday, Judas also led those brethren who, rejoicing, had asked him to receive the seal of our Lord also. And he went out to a spring of water, and he took oil[280] and gave praise over it, and he said:[281]

84

30:2*"We praise you, O mystery of salvation,*
which was given to us in oil by grace for anointing.

30:3*Glory to you, O hidden mystery,*
which was given to us in oil by grace for salvation,
for anointing.

Glory to you, O hidden mystery,
which was given to us in oil for salvation and
absolution.

30:4*And by it*[282] *(you) enlighten us and drive away*
darkness and error from us.

And again, by its mystery the athletes of the contest
defeat their enemies.

30:5*Glory to you, O mystery of the oil,*
since you became worthy to be in fellowship with
Christ.

With you the victorious are crowned in the contest,
and you are twinned with the Spirit.

^{30:6}*And you fly over the water like your (twin,)*
the Holy Spirit,
you mix the soul with mind,
and you renew the body with the birth of salvation.

^{30:7}*Come, O partner of the firstborn;*

Come, O renewer of humanity by the birth to eternal
life;

^{30:8}*and rest upon these believers, the beloved ones of our*
Lord Jesus Christ, and purify them and sanctify them
from all the stains of their bodies,

^{30:9}*and may they become for you temples for your*
dwelling
and rest for the Son of perfect mercy.

And may you perfectly sanctify them with the birth of
salvation."

31. THE MAGI RECEIVE THE EUCHARIST AND COMMISSION TO PREACH

^{31:1}And he baptized them in the name of the Father and the Son and the Holy Spirit,[283] and when they all came up from the water, a certain child of heavenly light appeared to them, who descended from heaven and said to them: "Peace be with you, sons of all my mysteries.[284] And behold, now all the visions and revelations that you

saw from the first day have been accomplished in your birth." [31:2]And they were afraid and fell upon the ground,[285] and when they stood up he appeared to them in the form of a glorious and divine young man. And taking a whole loaf of bread, he gave praise, broke, and gave first to the Apostle Judas, and also to each one of them, and he said to them, "Behold the consummation and sealing of your birth of salvation. From now and forever, be confirmed in my promise." [31:3]And when he was separated from their sight, again they saw him going up to heaven in glory that has no end. [31:4]And Judas said: "We glorify your sweet majesty, your singularity in many personifications, your glorious images that you have shown us, and the clothes that you have put on for our sake, that we may be clothed in your powerful majesty. [31:5]And by as many names as you have been called, you are not in any one of them, for you alone have known your great name[286] and your majesty, and your exalted Father, and no one else. [31:6]And all these forms in which you were clothed and appeared for our sake, that we might know you, were because you loved us with your great mercy that was for us, and everything that the crucifiers brought upon you, you endured for our sake, being exalted above all sufferings and being a kinsperson of that one who does not suffer,[287] in order that we should have redemption by your grace. [31:7]And on our behalf you endured everything and you suffered everything, for you are our advocate, and our guide, and our light, and our savior, and because we have believed in you, we have everything in you. And you have completely given it to us by the trust of your love toward us, you who endured everything for our sake." [31:8]And all the new disciples of the word of salvation answered and said with great joy: "We glorify, and we worship, and we give thanks for your majesty, which is unspeakable by the mouth of human beings because we are too weak for it, and for your great light, you caused to shine upon our weakness, by which you made us worthy in your mercy for your fellowship of everlasting life." [31:9]And while they were delighting greatly in thanksgiving, and prayer, and visions of our Lord, a multitude of brethren were added to the faith day by day.[288] [31:10]And Judas said to them: "Therefore, my brethren, let us fulfill the commandment of our Lord, who said to us: 'Go out into the entire world and preach my Gospel.'[289] So, my brethren, be you also preachers of the Word like us, because you have also received the gift of our Lord. Also go out to every place and preach the gift of our light and of our savior generously to everyone."

32. THE PREACHING OF THE MAGI

[32:1]And they[290] went forth from there to every place and preached in perfect love about the coming of our Lord

Jesus Christ, the Son of the Lord of all, even doing mighty works and healings in the name of our Lord, which are unspeakable by the mouth of human beings, through the Holy Spirit that was poured out upon them by the gift of our Lord. [32:2]And they preached the faith of truth, saying and teaching to everyone: "Flee from the darkness and come to the light that does not pass away, so that you may live and have refuge under the wings[291] of our Lord Jesus, our savior and our great refuge on the last day, from the fearsome judgment of fire that will come suddenly to purify the entire earth from error,[292] which has ruled over it in its deceit. [32:3]And you shall be delivered by faith from the heat of the fire and shall enter that rest that is prepared for all the chosen and the believers who have believed in the child of perfect light, and in eternal life, in the kingdom of my[293] Lord Jesus Christ, the Son of the Lord of all, in his heavenly majesty, in his new world, and in his heavenly and great and never-passing-away light, and in his glorious rest. And you shall rest forever and ever, amen and amen." [32:4]The story about the Magi and their gifts has finished.[294]

Ꮯꜧe Ꮇeanings of the "Revelation of the Ꮇagi"

W hat are the most important things we learn from the *Revelation of the Magi?* Is it merely a colorful and captivating piece of fiction? Or does it tell us anything about the Magi and the Christmas story that we wouldn't otherwise know? What might be the broader significance of this ancient tale—not just for scholars who specialize in early Christianity, but for a wide range of lay readers as well?

Two points especially come to mind. First, the *Revelation of the Magi* is an outstanding example of how much influence writings *outside of* the Bible can have on our conceptions of biblical texts, people, and events. Of course, some readers may deny that their understandings of the Bible are determined by anything other than the Bible itself. But to illustrate how apocryphal writings can shape our views of biblical stories, I'd like you to ask yourself this question: in the Christmas story, how do Mary and Joseph get to Bethlehem?

I would imagine that many of you said that they used a donkey. Indeed, some of you may have been more specific: that Mary rode the donkey while Joseph walked. But take a look at Luke 2:1–7, the most famous account of the Christmas story and of the census that brought Mary and Joseph to Bethlehem.

> In those days a decree went out from Emperor Augustus that all the world should be registered. This was the first registration and was taken while Quirinius was governor of Syria. All went to their own towns to be registered. Joseph also went from the town of Nazareth in Galilee to Judea, to the city of David called Bethlehem, because he was descended from the house and family of David. He went to be registered with Mary, to whom he was engaged and who was expecting a child. While they were there, the time came for her to deliver her child. And she gave birth to her firstborn son and wrapped him in bands of cloth, and laid him in a manger, because there was no place for them in the inn.

Conclusion

Do you see the familiar donkey mentioned anywhere? Why isn't it mentioned? The reality is that although it has become common knowledge that Mary and Joseph used a donkey to get to Bethlehem, this information isn't found anywhere in Luke or, in fact, in the rest of the Bible.

The famous donkey first appears in the *Protevangelium of James*, a second-century apocryphal Infancy Gospel. Here is what that writing says:

> He [i.e., Joseph] saddled the donkey and seated her [i.e., Mary] on it; and his son led it along, while Joseph followed behind. (*Protevangelium of James* 17:2)

From its debut in the *Protevangelium*, the donkey appeared in other ancient retellings of the Christmas story, and from there to Christmas pageants, greeting cards, carols, and so forth—despite its never being mentioned at all in the Bible! Might the *Revelation of the Magi*, like the *Protevangelium*, also have elements that have influenced our understanding of the Christmas story?

To my knowledge, there is nothing in the *Revelation of the Magi* that has filtered into the version of the Christmas story that we know *today*, certainly not like the donkey has. Yet the *Revelation of the Magi* has not always been as invisible as it is now. In fact, for European

Christians in the Middle Ages and the Renaissance, this story had an immense influence.

How did the *Revelation of the Magi*, an ancient Syriac writing, become such a powerful influence in medieval and Renaissance Europe? Recall that in the introduction, I mentioned a summary of the *Revelation of the Magi* found in the *Opus Imperfectum in Matthaeum*, a fifth-century Latin commentary on the Gospel of Matthew. When I discussed it before, its significance was as a key witness to the *Revelation of the Magi*, helping us to learn how old the text actually might be. But my very brief mention of the *Opus Imperfectum* does not do justice to how influential this text became in the centuries after which it was composed.

We don't know who wrote the *Opus Imperfectum;* all we can infer is that it was written in the fifth century and that the author lived somewhere close to the great city of Constantinople. But for reasons unknown, it became incorrectly attributed to Saint John Chrysostom, a major Christian thinker and bishop in fourth-century Antioch. Because it was believed to have been penned by Chrysostom, the *Opus Imperfectum* continued to be copied and read throughout medieval Europe.

And this meant that its legend about the Magi also entered the world of medieval Christianity. Several pieces of artwork are reproduced in this book that show unquestionable influence from the *Revelation of the*

Magi. Consider the two paintings associated with Rogier van der Weyden and his school, which today reside in the Gemäldegalerie in Berlin and the Cloisters Museum in New York, respectively (see frontispiece and page 51). In each of these, the three Magi stand in awe of the Christ child, who prominently hovers above them in the form of a star! As I said in the introduction, the *Revelation of the Magi* is the only ancient Christian text to identify the Star of Bethlehem with the celestial Christ himself, which makes it virtually certain that this legend is the source of these paintings. Further details confirm this. Behind the Magi stands their sacred mountain, the Mountain of Victories. And in the Cloisters painting, the Magi again appear in the background, immersing themselves in their Spring of Purification. The influence of the *Revelation of the Magi* is also evident in the depictions of the Magi found in manuscripts and printed books of the *Speculum Humanae Salvationis* (Mirror of Human Salvation), an immensely popular devotional writing of the fourteenth century (see *Speculum Humanae Salvationis* on pages 40 and 41).

Apart from inspiring artistic representations of the Magi, this legend also captivated Christian thinkers as distinguished as Saint Thomas Aquinas. In the *Summa Theologica,* his greatest work, Aquinas uses the *Revelation of the Magi* as evidence that the Star of Bethlehem was a clear and unmistakable way for God to tell human beings about the birth of Christ. Even if the meaning of the star wasn't obvious to everyone, it certainly was to the Magi, who knew about its coming through Seth's books of revelation and were waiting attentively for it.[295]

The *Revelation of the Magi* even influenced the way explorers of the New World understood the indigenous cultures they encountered (see *Adoration of the Magi* on page 95). Two examples will suffice. First, there is the seventeenth-century Augustinian monk Antonio de la Calancha, who studied the Incan culture of Peru. He was impressed by the similarities between Andean traditional religion and Christianity, and he believed that the Apostle Thomas and the Magi must have missionized the region together, just as the *Opus Imperfectum* indicated.[296] Second, the Franciscan missionary and historian Juan de Torquemada described the belief among some of the Aztecs that the conquistador Cortés was the god Quetzalcoatl with recourse to this legend. Just as the Magi had stood atop the Mountain of Victories awaiting

Adoration of the Magi, attributed to Vasco Fernandes, Museu Nacional de Arte Antiga, Lisbon, Portugal. This early-sixteenth-century painting represents one of the three Magi as a Native American. Both the biblical story of the Magi and the *Revelation of the Magi* influenced the ways in which explorers of the New World interpreted indigenous cultures of the Americas.

the fulfillment of their prophecy, Torquemada notes, so, too, did the Aztecs anxiously await the foretold return of Quetzalcoatl, and were all too willing to accept Cortés as the returned Quetzalcoatl when Spanish ships appeared off the Mexican coast.

So the legend found in the *Revelation of the Magi* was demonstrably important for Christians in Europe half a millennium ago. And it is a powerful example of the way that an apocryphal writing can strongly influence understandings of biblical events, even if it does not figure into the portrayal of the "Wise Men" in the Christmas story as we know it today.

But as my second and final remark, I want to suggest a different reason that the *Revelation of the Magi* may be especially relevant for today's world. Speaking for a moment as a theologian rather than a historian, I think that the most important thing about the *Revelation of the Magi* may not be what it says about the Magi, but what it says about *Christ.*

Recall that in the introduction I asked the question of why the *Revelation of the Magi* has been so neglected by modern scholars of early Christianity that it has only now been translated into English. The answer I gave there was that it had the misfortune of being preserved in a language few scholars knew, and of being part of not one but *two* neglected spheres of early Christian literature—stories about Jesus's birth, and writings that were not included in the New Testament.

But one might as willingly believe, if so inclined, that the introduction of the *Revelation of the Magi* to a wide audience at this precise moment in time is hardly a matter of chance. As already discussed, the *Revelation of the Magi* has a very unusual understanding of the origins of the world's religious traditions. Instead of seeing non-Christian religions as products of human vanity or demonic inspiration, as most ancient Christians did, the *Revelation of the Magi* sees potentially all revelation as coming from Christ himself. Moreover, because the star-child never reveals himself to the Magi as Christ, the *Revelation of the Magi* apparently believes that having *an experience of Christ's presence* is much more important than *being a Christian.*

Taking this radical viewpoint, the *Revelation of the Magi* practically stands alone among early Christian writings in its positive appraisal of religious pluralism. So, another way of answering the question of why the *Revelation of the Magi* is now beginning to be studied more closely is that such a text could be fully appreciated *only* in a moment such as today. Now more than ever before, religious diversity is a fact of life in many parts of the world. And this religious diversity has given birth, in recent decades, to a great deal of theological reflection on

the place of Christianity among the world's religious traditions. It has become more intellectually challenging to
insist on the obvious and exclusive truth of one's religion
when one lives and works in close proximity to other
people who cherish their own religious tradition just as
much. Are those who do not share our religious beliefs
foolishly misguided? According to the *Revelation of the
Magi*, the answer of Christ to the Magi appears to be no:

> And I am everywhere, because I am a ray of
> light whose light has shone in this world from
> the majesty of my Father, who has sent me to
> fulfill everything that was spoken about me
> in the entire world and in every land by un-
> speakable mysteries, and to accomplish the
> commandment of my glorious Father, who by
> the prophets preached about me to the con-
> tentious house,[297] in the same way as for you,
> as befits your faith, it was revealed to you
> about me. (13:10)

ACKNOWLEDGMENTS

————

Many people have helped me to bring the *Revelation of the Magi* to a wider audience. My work on this text started during my doctoral program at Harvard Divinity School. I am grateful to my thesis adviser, Professor François Bovon, for his careful shepherding of this project from its inception, and his kindness in introducing me to the scholarly community in Europe that is devoted to the study of early Christian apocryphal literature. Professor J. F. Coakley, now of the University of Cambridge, spent countless hours supervising my translation of the *Revelation of the Magi* from the Syriac. His very patient editing of my work has saved me from embarrassment time and again, and any errors remaining in the translation are entirely my own. Professor Karen King consistently pushed me toward further analytical rigor during the dissertation-writing process. Other colleagues from Harvard who have provided helpful advice on innumerable occasions include Ellen Aitken, Carly Daniel-Hughes, Ben Dunning, Ken Fisher, Anne-Marie

99

Acknowledgments

Luijendijk, and Laura Nasrallah, as well as innumerable other faculty members and graduate students who offered constructive feedback during seminars and workshops. I am very grateful to the following faculty members for being extremely supportive of my professional development: Susan Abraham, Nicola Denzey, Eldon Epp, Helmut Koester, Anne Monius, and Stephanie Paulsell. I would also like to single out for special thanks Margaret Studier, managing editor of *Harvard Theological Review*, who urged me to submit my dissertation to Harper Collins to be considered for the Huston Smith Prize.

My new colleagues at the University of Oklahoma have also provided invaluable support, particularly as I worked toward adapting the work of my dissertation for a more general audience. I am especially grateful to Erik Braun, Rangar Cline, Marie Dallam, Kyle Harper, Rachel Knudsen, Rienk Vermij, David Vishanoff, and Jane Wickersham for their feedback. I am especially grateful to my program director, Dr. Charles Kimball, for his strong support of this project in my first year of teaching. I am indebted to the senior members of the Religious Studies Program, Tom and Barbara Boyd, for their kind encouragement and support of me as a newcomer to Oklahoma.

I am exceedingly grateful to Eric Brandt at Harper Collins for his resolute support of my work. His enthusiasm for the *Revelation of the Magi* has buoyed the project

Acknowledgments

through the planning and editing stages. Thanks to him, the final form of this book is far better than I could have ever imagined. I am very thankful to his assistant, Kathryn Renz, for her kindness and accessibility in explaining various aspects of the publishing process to me, as a first-time author. I am also indebted to the careful editing of Carolyn Holland and Carl Walesa, and to the design talents of Janet Evans.

My family has been my deepest source of inspiration and support. My father, Greg; my mother, Debby; my sister, Elizabeth; and my brother, Brian, and his wife, Leslie, have all encouraged me with their enthusiasm for this project, as have my father-in-law, Bill Bangs, and brother-in-law, Jonathan Bangs. I would especially like to thank my mother-in-law, Margie Bangs, who constituted a crucial focus group of one for my translation and introduction. My grandmother, Helen Mason, and my uncle, H. D. Mitchell, were both eager to read whatever I sent them and put their theological training to good use. Finally, my deepest love, admiration, and gratitude are for my wife, Elizabeth, who is both my toughest critic and biggest fan.

The Magi Legend from the "Opus Imperfectum in Matthaeum"

[The Latin text of the *Opus Imperfectum in Matthaeum* is taken from Migne's *Patrologia Graeca,* volume 56, columns 637–638. It can also be found, with translation and commentary, in chapter 2 of my dissertation, available online at http://ou.academia.edu/BrentLandau/Papers.]

Apocryphal Book Under the Name of Seth. Victorious Mountain.—I have heard some referring to such a writing, even if it is not beyond dispute, nevertheless not ruining the faith, but charming (it), seeing that there was a certain race situated at the very beginning of the East near the Ocean, who had possession of a certain writing having been inscribed with the name of Seth, concerning this star which was going to appear, and (concerning) what sort of gifts to offer it, which was carried out through generations of studious people, with the fathers handing down to their sons. And so they selected from themselves twelve more learned ones and lovers of the celestial mysteries, and they set before them the expectation of that star. And if someone from them died, his son or one of his relatives who was found of the same inclination was set up in place of the dead one. And they were called Magi in their language, because in silence and with a silent voice they glorified God. Therefore, during every year, after the threshing harvest, they went up a certain mountain placed there, which was called in their language the Victorious Mountain, having in it a certain cave in the rock, most pleasant, with fountains and choice trees, going up into which, and washing themselves, they were praying and glorifying God in silence for three days. And they did thus for each generation, always waiting, that by chance in their generation that star of blessing might appear, until it appeared to them coming down above that Victorious Mountain, having in itself a form like a little boy and above it (or him?) the likeness of a cross. And it was speaking to them, and it taught them and instructed them to set out for Judaea. And while they journeyed for two years, the star went ahead, and neither food nor drink ran out from their pouches. And otherwise the deeds that were rendered by them were expressed in the compendious Gospel. However, when they had returned,

Appendix

they continued worshiping and glorifying God even more attentively than before, and they preached to all in their race, and they instructed many. Finally, after the Resurrection of the Lord, when the Apostle Thomas went into that province, they joined him, and having been baptized by him, they were made assistants of his preaching.

Frontispiece: Rogier (Roger) van der Weyden (ca. 1399–1464) (workshop of): The star in the form of a Child appears to the three Magi. Right wing of the Middleburg (Bladelin) Altarpiece. Ca. 1445. Berlin, Gemäldegalerie. Oil on oak panel. Detail. 91 x 40 cm. Inv.: 535. Photo: Joerg P. Anders. Photo Credit : Bildarchiv Preussischer Kulturbesitz / Art Resource, NY

(Pages 4 and 5) *The Three Kings (Wise Men)*. Early Christian mosaic. 6th century C.E. S. Apollinare Nuovo, Ravenna, Italy. Photo Credit : Scala / Art Resource, NY

(Page 14) *Adoration of the Magi*. 5th century C.E. Early Christian. Cypress wood carving from the door. S. Sabina, Rome, Italy. Photo Credit : Alinari / Art Resource, NY

(Page 27) Benozzo Gozzoli (1420–1497) *The Adoration of the Magi* (with Gozzoli's self-portrait—with red cap). Lorenzo il Magnifico as the youngest of the three Magi. Fresco, 1459. Palazzo Medici Riccardi, Florence, Italy. Photo Credit : Erich Lessing / Art Resource, NY

(Pages 40 and 41) *The Three Magi. Speculum Humanae Salvationis*, by Ludolfus de Saxonia. Ms.15, f.10r. Vellum. Germany, ca. 1410. Spencer Collection. Astor, Lenox and Tilden Foundations. Photo Credit : New York Public Library / Art Resource, NY

(Page 51) Rogier van der Weyden, Follower of. Polyptych. Mid-15th century. Tempera and oil. Main Panel: 33 3/16 x 55 1/8 in. (84.3 x 140 cm); Upper Wings: 17 15/16 x 7 7/8 in. (45.6 x 20 cm); Lower Wings: 33 5/8 x 16 5/8 in. (85.4 x 42.2 cm). South Lowlands, Brabant, Brussels. The Metropolitan Museum of Art, the Cloisters Collection, 1949 (49.109). Photo credit: Image copyright © The Metropolitan Museum of Art / Art Resource, NY

(Pages 62 and 63) Sassetta (Stefano di Giovanni) (ca. 1400–1450) *The Journey of the Magi.* Ca. 1435. Tempera and gold on wood, 8 1/2 x 11 3/4 in. (21.6 x 29.8 cm). Maitland F. Griggs Collection, Bequest of Maitland F. Griggs, 1943 (43.98.1). The Metropolitan Museum of Art, NY. Photo Credit: Image copyright © The Metropolitan Museum of Art / Art Resource, NY

(Page 95) Vasco Fernandes (ca. 1480–ca. 1543) *Adoration of the Magi.* Museu Nacional de Arte Antiga, Lisbon, Portugal. Photo Credit: Scala /White Images / Art Resource, NYT8829

(Endpapers) MS Vaticanus Syriacus 162 ©2010, Biblioteca Apostolica Vaticana, all rights reserved

---

1. The names Balthazar, Caspar, and Melchior are most familiar to Westerners, but these names appear in written sources from only the sixth century onward. Several other lists of names survive from ancient Christian writings.

2. Going forward, I will prefer the term *Magi* to *wise men.* First of all, it respects what Matthew calls them, since it is simply a transliteration of the Greek *magoi.* Second, it leaves unresolved the question of precisely *who* these individuals are, since it is not at all clear who Matthew believed them to be. Leaving the question of their identity open-ended is important, since early Christians had a range of theories about their identity; the story addressed in this book has its own very distinct understanding of who the Magi were.

3. For other uses of the noun and its cognate verb, see Acts 8:9, 13:6, 8.

4. Matthew's Gospel never specifies whether the star had led them to Jerusalem and then disappeared when they entered the city, or whether the Magi had seen it only initially in "the East." In either case, Mt 2:9–10 seems to imply that the star had disappeared from the Magi for some period of time.

5. All three of these beliefs appear in early Christian literature. One story relates that the Magi were in the midst of

their magical spells at the time of the star's appearance; when the spells ceased to work, they consulted their ancient prophecies and learned about the star (see Origen *Against Celsus* 1.60). Some members of John Chrysostom's congregation in fourth-century Antioch regarded the Magi as astrologers and believed (to his great frustration) that the Magi story showed that astrology really worked (*Homilies on Matthew* 6.1). Lastly, an ancient Infancy Gospel preserved in Arabic says that the Magi came to Jerusalem because of a prophecy of Zoroaster, the founder of their religion (*Arabic Infancy Gospel* 7).

6. Precisely when the star disappeared is unclear, just as in Matthew's Gospel.

7. In their book on the infancy narratives, Marcus Borg and John Dominic Crossan demonstrate these differences quite well by showing what a Christmas pageant based on only Matthew or only Luke would look like. See Borg and Crossan, *The First Christmas: What the Gospels Really Teach About Jesus's Birth* (San Francisco: HarperOne, 2007), 3–24.

8. Two recent scholars have argued for the historicity of some aspects of the infancy narratives. Jane Schaberg, in her *Illegitimacy of Jesus: A Feminist Theological Interpretation of the Infancy Narratives* (Revised edition, Sheffield, UK: Sheffield Phoenix, 2006), asserts that the detail that Jesus was conceived outside of wedlock is historical, though she does not specify who she believes his father was. Not surprisingly, Schaberg's claim is quite controversial and has not been accepted by many scholars. Andries van Aarde, in his *Fatherless in Galilee: Jesus as Child of God* (Harrisburg, PA: Trinity, 2001), suggests that the presence of Joseph in the infancy narratives and his corresponding absence during Jesus's adulthood indicates that Joseph died when Jesus was quite young, leaving Jesus to grow up without a father figure.

Notes

9. The small number of scholars who investigated the *Revelation of the Magi* in the twentieth century mainly regarded the text as the product of Zoroastrian converts to Christianity in Iran, written with the goal of reconciling their ancestral religious tradition with their new Christian identity. Although this theory is quite intriguing, I have not found it to be at all persuasive. It is not possible to treat this issue in the very limited space of an introduction; however, the basic fact that these Magi live in the mythical land of Shir—not Persia—is one powerful indication that the *Revelation of the Magi* has nothing to do with Zoroastrianism.

10. For example, no original copies of any of the writings of the New Testament exist. The earliest copy of a New Testament writing is a tiny papyrus fragment of the Gospel of John, usually dated to 125–150 C.E. (The Gospel itself was most likely written in 90–100 C.E.) Apart from this fragment, the earliest copies of New Testament writings are from the late second and early third centuries or later.

11. Theodore bar Konai tells us that the Magi arrived in Jerusalem during the month of April—a rather odd claim, given that practically all ancient Christians celebrated the arrival of the Magi (Epiphany) in early January. The only other ancient Christian writing that claims that the Magi came to Jerusalem in April is none other than the *Revelation of the Magi*.

12. A translation of the *Opus Imperfectum*'s summary of the *Revelation of the Magi* is found in the appendix.

13. The author knows that the Magi's name in their language refers to their practice of silent prayer, that the sacred mountain of the Magi is called the "Victorious Mountain" (as opposed to "Mountain of Victories" in the Syriac text), and that this mountain has a cave, a fountain, and trees (though the placement of these features differs slightly in the two witnesses).

14. Most notably, the Apostle Thomas section of the *Revelation of the Magi* contains a baptismal hymn sung by Thomas that invokes the Holy Spirit; several similar hymns exist in the Acts of Thomas. The account of the Magi's baptism also shares a number of parallels with baptismal scenes in the Acts of Thomas. But it is important to emphasize that these are parallels of *form,* not *content:* the *Revelation of the Magi* and the Acts of Thomas do not share any narrative elements.

15. This is because the Apostle Thomas section of the *Revelation of the Magi* appears to have been written in direct response to what is said in the first-person section of the *Revelation of the Magi* and would not have circulated separately.

16. In fact, as Raymond E. Brown has noted in *The Birth of the Messiah: A Commentary on the Infancy Narratives in the Gospels of Matthew and Luke* (2nd ed.; New York: Doubleday, 1993), belief in the historicity of the Magi story has, in the recent past, been used as an indicator of whether a scholar was inside or outside of the mainstream of biblical studies.

17. Of course, there have been numerous attempts to link the Star of Bethlehem to a supernova, comet, or other celestial phenomenon. But these attempts almost always fail to recognize that the behavior that Matthew attributes to the star—especially its ability to mark the direct spot of the child Jesus in Mt 2:9—cannot occur in any natural fashion.

18. If we assume that that Jesus was born in approximately 4 B.C.E. (the most common date estimated by scholars) and that the Magi visited Jesus shortly thereafter, more than fifty years would pass before Paul wrote his earliest letters, which are the earliest Christian writings we possess.

19. The most famous of the apocryphal Infancy Gospels are the *Protevangelium of James,* which focuses more on the up-bringing of Mary than Jesus, and the *Infancy Gospel of Thomas,* famous for its depiction of Jesus as a vindictive child possessing frequently deadly miraculous powers. The Infancy Gospel that the *Revelation of the Magi* has used is preserved in medieval Latin and Irish manuscripts and is a lengthy expansion and harmonization of the materials found in the canonical infancy narratives, plus a number of traditions not found elsewhere.

20. This name is on the analogy of "Planet X," a designation coined by the astronomer Percival Lowell (the namesake of Flagstaff's Lowell Observatory) for an unknown planet beyond the orbit of Neptune—a hypothesis that, although flawed in some respects, ultimately led to the discovery of the planet Pluto. Although the name *"Infancy Gospel X"* is by no means ideal, unfortunately so little work has been done on this text that no more descriptive name presents itself.

21. For more discussion of the number of the Magi, see the note at 16:2 in the translation.

22. Pseudonymity, or the practice of writing under a false name, is acknowledged by most scholars to describe the authorship of many New Testament writings. This includes all four canonical Gospels (even if some scholars believe that the nucleus of one or more of the Gospels ultimately goes back to the name associated with the text) and roughly half of the letters attributed to Paul (even if some of the spurious letters perhaps contain authentic Pauline fragments).

23. I assume here that the author was male simply because of the much higher literacy rate of men as compared with women in the ancient world. But none of my arguments about the purpose of the *Revelation of the Magi* necessarily demand male authorship.

24. The most famous sending forth of the disciples to worldwide evangelism is the so-called Great Commission of Mt 28:18–20: "All authority in heaven and on earth has been given to me. Go therefore and make disciples of all nations, baptizing them in the name of the Father and of the Son and of the Holy Spirit, and teaching them to obey everything that I have commanded you. And remember, I am with you always, to the end of the age."

25. In fact, a number of early Christian writers were uncomfortable with Matthew's Magi story precisely because it did not indicate that their visit to Christ had altered their lives in any fashion. One commentator, Tertullian (*On Idolatry* 9), solved this problem by understanding Matthew's phrase "they departed to their own country by another way" (Mt 2:12) to mean that they had converted to faith in Christ.

26. These accompanying notes are intended to aid readers in understanding the basic meaning and significance of important passages in the *Revelation of the Magi*. For greater detail and analysis, please consult my dissertation (available online at http://ou.academia.edu/BrentLandau/Papers) and my forthcoming critical edition of the *Revelation of the Magi* for the Corpus Christianorum Series Apocryphorum, published by Brepols.

27. The titles of the individual chapters are my own, and do not appear in the manuscript of the *Chronicle of Zuqnin* (the Syriac world chronicle in which the *Revelation of the Magi* is preserved). Only two symbols in the text require comment. In places where the manuscript has suffered damage, square brackets [ ] contain what I consider to be the most likely original reading. In places where it is impossible to determine the original reading, square brackets simply contain the words *text missing*. In contrast, parentheses ( ) indicate places where a word or words have been added to clarify the meaning of the text beyond a literal translation of the Syriac.

28. The short descriptive statement contained in 1:1 is the work of the compiler of the *Chronicle of Zuqnin*, not the author of the *Revelation of the Magi.* This is certain not only from the appearance of such statements elsewhere in the *Chronicle,* but also because this statement misrepresents the *Revelation of the Magi* in two important ways. First, the statement emphasizes the gifts that the Magi bring, but the *Revelation of the Magi* cares much less about these gifts than the canonical account of Mt 2:1–12 does. Second, the statement uses the proper name *Christ,* but this name is used only during the Apostle Thomas's appearance at the end of the *Revelation of the Magi,* an incident that is most likely a secondary addition to the *Revelation of the Magi.*

29. The association of the Magi with royalty began quite early in Christian exegesis, perhaps thanks to such suggestive passages as Ps 72:10–11 and Is 60. Tertullian (*Against Marcion* 3.13) remarks that in the East, the Magi are treated practically as kings. For Augustine in the fourth century, they are definitely kings, and their piety is contrasted against King Herod's impiousness (*Sermon* 200). However, in the first-person-plural section of the *Revelation of the Magi,* there is almost no mention of their royal status. The term *king* never appears in reference to the Magi; the only indication that the Magi are kings occurs at 18:5, where they remove their crowns and lay them at Christ's feet in recognition of his kingdom.

30. The phrase "kings, sons of kings" is how Syriac writers describe hereditary kingship, as compared with the inconsistent manner of succession found in the Roman Empire.

31. The residence of the Magi here derives, unsurprisingly, from Mt 2:1. Throughout the *Revelation of the Magi,* however, it appears that "East" is not simply directional, but has the status of a specific nation with a corresponding ethnic group (cf. "Easterners" in 24:4). There are nine such usages of "East" in the *Revelation of the Magi* (in addition to three directional instances), though the name "Shir" (2:4 and corresponding note; 4:1) also appears in the *Revelation of the Magi* as the land of the Magi. It may be that the "great East" is understood in the *Revelation of the Magi* as a quite large country or region, of which Shir is the outermost district, as 2:4 seems to imply.

32. This statement reveals the *Revelation of the Magi* as a pseudepigraphon (i.e., a writing that makes false claims about the identity of its author), stating as it does that it was produced by the Magi themselves. No other Magi pseudepigrapha are known to exist from antiquity, and this is one of only a handful of cases where Christians produced writings purported to have been authored by non-Christians.

33. According to the *Revelation of the Magi*, the word *Magi* is related etymologically to their practice of praying in silence, which the text mentions on several other occasions (cf. 1:3, 2:1, 3:8, 5:7, 5:11, 12:2). Yet, a verbal similarity between the words *Magi* and *silence* is not easy to find in any of the obvious languages of transmission (Syriac, Greek, or Latin). It may simply be an exoticizing device and not an actual word derivation. Strikingly, the *Opus Imperfectum in Matthaeum* (the fifth-century Latin commentary on the Gospel of Matthew that contains a brief version of this same legend about the Magi) agrees with the *Revelation of the Magi* in almost verbatim fashion on this point: "And they were called Magi in their language, because in silence and with a silent voice they glorified God." This close agreement suggests that the author of the *Opus Imperfectum* had not simply heard of this legend, but also had access to a written version of the *Revelation of the Magi*. In a number of Syriac monastic writings, silence is a means for inducing ecstasy. Unlike these monastic traditions, though, the *Revelation of the Magi* nowhere suggests that the silent praying of the Magi facilitates ecstatic experience. It has sometimes been thought that Zoroastrian priests prayed in silence, but other scholars have rejected this view. A hagiographic Syriac text, the *Life of John of Tella*, relates that the Magi frequently convey information to one another in silence by using hand gestures. However, this is not in the context of prayer, but rather the interrogation of a prisoner.

34. This title for God is used infrequently in Jewish and Christian literature (cf. 2 Mc 14:46). However, it does appear in Babylonian, Zoroastrian, and Hindu materials from antiquity. Though it is very difficult to prove that the author of *Revelation of the Magi* knew of its use in any of these written materials, the fact that it had a reasonably wide currency in non-Christian religious traditions may explain its use here. One of the major agendas of the author is the depiction of the Magi as a kind of quasi-pagan group that nevertheless distantly echoes Christian terminology and practice.

35. The "gift" is an important theological concept in the *Revelation of the Magi*, mentioned on multiple occasions throughout the text. In the abstract, it is the mechanism by which an unknowable God communicates with the inhabitants of the upper and lower worlds. In a concrete sense, it refers specifically to the revelatory activity of Christ. The Syriac term underlying this concept must be distinguished from the other term used for "gift" in the *Revelation of the Magi*, which refers to the offerings brought to Christ by the Magi (Mt 2:11; see note at 4:7). The New Testament, like the *Revelation of the Magi*, generally uses the abstract sense of the term, describing the "gift" of the Holy Spirit, Christ, or God (cf. Jn 4:10; Acts 2:38, 8:20, 10:45, 11:17; Rom 5:15–17; 2 Cor 9:15; Eph 3:7, 4:7; Heb 6:4; Jas 1:17).

36. The *Revelation of the Magi* is one of only a handful of ancient texts to refer to the Magi as "wise." For the most part, the familiar description of the Magi as "wise men" appears only from the Renaissance onward.

37. Cf. Jn 1:3.

38. In the development of traditions about the Magi, the attribution of names to them is a relatively late exegetical development. The most familiar names in the West for the (three) Magi are Caspar, Melchior, and Balthazar, but these names appear only in the sixth century in the *Excerpta Latina Barbari*, a Latin translation of a Greek chronicle. As for the names found in the *Revelation of the Magi*, I have incorporated without changes the spelling of the names as found in the Latin translation accompanying the most recent critical edition of the *Chronicle of Zuqnin*. The names play no further role in the *Revelation of the Magi*'s narrative beyond this single mention, and their presence in other Syriac sources strongly suggests that 2:3 is a later accretion to the *Revelation of the Magi*. In a peculiar case of interrelation, the *Revelation of the Magi* has a *list* of the Magi numbering twelve, but nowhere explicitly does it say that there are *twelve* Magi, whereas the *Opus Imperfectum in Matthaeum* does state that there were twelve Magi, *without* giving a list of names. The information of the *Opus Imperfectum* is perhaps more archaic, and specific names may have been given to the twelve Magi only at a later time (but cf. 16:2 and accompanying note for a possibly even earlier tradition of a larger, numerically unspecified membership for the ranks of the Magi).

39. The name "Gudaphar" is almost identical to "Gûdnaphar" (Gundaphorus), an Indian king baptized by the Apostle Thomas in the Acts of Thomas. The Acts of Thomas is the earliest written source that narrates Thomas's missionary activities in India. Although King Gûdnaphar appears to have been a historical figure, it is unclear whether he was indeed ruling at the time that the Apostle Thomas is supposed to have been in India—a very contentious debate in and of itself.

40. In contrast to the "land of the East," the name "Shir" is less common in the *Revelation of the Magi*, used only twice. However, it appears in a number of other ancient texts as a mysterious and faraway land, sometimes identified with China. In one of the Gnostic Christian texts discovered at Nag Hammadi, "Mount Shir" is the place where Noah's ark comes to rest; more remotely, "Mount Nisir" is where the ark of Utnapishtim lands in the *Epic of Gilgamesh*. The *Revelation of the Magi* is the only ancient Christian text that identifies the homeland of the Magi as Shir. The majority opinion of ancient commentators was that the Magi came from Persia, understanding the term *Magus* in its technical sense of a Zoroastrian priest; cf. Clement of Alexandria (*Miscellanies* 1.15); Origen (*Against Celsus* 1.58–60); John Chrysostom (*Homilies on Matthew* 6.2). Most early Christian artistic representations of the Magi also imply this, depicting them in the typical Persian dress of a pointed "Phrygian cap," belted tunic, and leggings; cf. especially the mosaic of Sant'Apollinare Nuovo in Ravenna (pages 4 and 5) and the wooden door detail of Santa Sabina in Rome (page 14). A notable and early minority opinion regarding the homeland of the Magi is Arabia; cf. Justin Martyr (*Dialogue with Trypho* 78, 106); Tertullian (*Against Marcion* 3.13, *Against the Jews* 9).

41. The concept of a great world ocean outside of the inhabited world had existed in antiquity at least as early as Homer. The location of the Magi's homeland in the *Opus Imperfectum in Matthaeum* is described in almost identical language: "situated at the very beginning of the East near the Ocean."

42. The precise geographical layout envisioned here is ambiguous; it is unclear whether the Ocean or Shir is east of the land of Nod. The most logical solution seems to be that that the Ocean is directly east of Shir, which is east of Nod.

43. Cf. Gn 4:16, though there it is the place of Cain's exile. Nod is mentioned very little in extrabiblical literature, and in no other cases does it appear to be the dwelling place of Adam.

44. I.e., "when Adam had Seth." The idea that Adam had received foreknowledge of the future and transmitted it to later generations through Seth or some other means occurs in numerous Jewish and Christian noncanonical writings. This understanding most likely derives from the incident of Adam eating from the Tree of Knowledge, which would have provided him with some sort of predictive ability.

45. Cf. Gn 3:23–24.

46. Mention of Seth's purity also appears in several other Jewish and Christian sources, and has implications for the character of his progeny. See Josephus *Antiquities* 1.68–69.

47. Cf. Gn 4:26 for the tradition that during the time of Seth and his son Enosh "people began to invoke the name of the LORD."

48. In claiming that Seth produced a written revelation, the *Revelation of the Magi* also has some general similarities with writings preserved in the Nag Hammadi corpus.

49. Cf. Gn 7:1.

50. This is the first instance of a phrase, "hidden mysteries," that occurs on twenty-one separate occasions in the *Revelation of the Magi*. Roughly half of these times it appears in the title "Cave of Treasures of Hidden Mysteries" (4:1); in this title and elsewhere it generally functions as the primary designation for the knowledge handed from Seth through the generations of Magi (but cf. 30:3, where it apparently refers to Christ).

51. Here it becomes clear that the narrators of the story are the

Magi themselves (or more precisely, the generation of Magi living at the time of Christ's coming). This first-person narration continues uninterrupted until 28:4, just prior to the arrival of the Apostle Thomas, where the text abruptly switches into third-person narration.

52. The praying posture of the Magi has analogues in ancient Jewish and Christian literature, even if it is not as well known as the *orans* position or other postures. It is most commonly mentioned in the Hebrew Bible; cf. 1 Kgs 8:54; 2 Chr 6:13; Ezr 9:5; Ps 68:31; Lam 3:41; 1 Tm 2:8.

53. The "Mountain of Victories" is paralleled in the *Opus Imperfectum in Matthaeum,* where it goes by a very similar name, "Victorious Mountain." The meaning of the name "Mountain of Victories / Victorious Mountain" is difficult to interpret, and several scholars have sought to connect it with one of several mountains associated with Zoroaster. However, these theories have little to commend to them. Holy mountains where theophanies take place are hardly a phenomenon exclusive to Zoroastrianism, and parallels to Jewish and Christian texts, such as Ex 24 and Mk 9:1–8, are perhaps more appropriate.

54. The "Cave of Treasures" also appears in a Syriac writing of the same name. The *Cave of Treasures* is a retelling of biblical history from the creation of the world through the coming of Christ, usually thought to have been written sometime between the fourth and sixth century C.E. In this work, the "Cave of Treasures" appears as the place of Adam's burial and as the repository of gifts that are brought by the Magi to Christ (*Cave of Treasures* 5.17, 6.22, 45.12). In the *Revelation of the Magi*, however, the primary importance of this cave is its housing of Seth's books of revelation, though the gifts are also mentioned, albeit briefly. Its usual title in the *Revelation of the Magi* is the "Cave of Treasures of Hidden Mysteries," but variants occur both here and in 4:2. The meaning of the phrase "the Mysteries of the Life of Silence" is not at all clear. It would seem to relate to the Magi's practice of silent prayer, yet the term "life of silence" is not found elsewhere in the *Revelation of the Magi*.

55. What follows is the prophecy of central importance for the descendants of Seth: the appearance of a star, and thus the manifestation of the Father's Son. The prophecy, like the rest of the *Revelation of the Magi* prior to 28:6, never mentions the name "Jesus" or "Christ," though allusions to Christian texts are frequent. This feature is part of the author's agenda to refer to Christian names and terminology only in an opaque manner. The idea that the Magi expect the star because of a prophecy going back to Seth is unparalleled in ancient Christian literature. According to Origen (*Against Celsus* 1.60; cf. also *Homilies on Numbers* 13.7, 18.4), the Magi were in the midst of magical practice when a luminous new star appeared and caused their spells to lose their efficacy, prompting them to consult the prophecy of their forefather Balaam from Nm 24:17. In *On the Star,* a composition falsely attributed to Eusebius of Caesarea, the Magi have been closely following the prophecies of Balaam, since they have proven true in the past, and hence they immediately recognize the appearance of the star as the fulfillment of another of Balaam's prophecies. Another pagan prophet who was thought to have predicted the events surrounding the star was Zoroaster. The *Arabic Infancy Gospel* 7:1 states that the Magi arrived in Jerusalem, "just as Zeradusht had predicted." Zoroaster also predicts the birth of Christ in a narrative preserved by the Syriac writer Theodore bar Konai.

56. Cf. Mt 2:2.

57. The information that the Magi are to expect a "light . . . in the form of a star," rather than simply a star, is significant, since the star is actually the preexistent Christ.

58. The precise role and symbolism of this "pillar of light" in the narrative is unclear. Although the *Revelation of the Magi* mentions the pillar upon which the star sits ten times, these mentions are always during the sequence when the star appears, descends from heaven, and stands before the mouth of a cave (either in Shir or in Bethlehem). Thus, the pillar has no explicit role as a guide for the Magi during their journey; only the star is named at this point in the story. But it is difficult to understand the significance of this pillar without recourse to the Exodus narrative; indeed, the scribe responsible for the text wrote "pillar of cloud" instead of "pillar of light" at a point late in the narrative (27:4). This is the only time this phrase appears in the *Revelation of the Magi* (elsewhere it is "pillar of light"), so it may be no more than a transmission error, but at the very least, it demonstrates a possible (if unintentional) reference to Exodus.

59. Cf. 11:5–7 (and accompanying note at 11:5), 16:4.

60. Cf. Col 1:15.

61. Cf. Jn 4:14.

62. The phrase "who sent" (usually followed by "me") appears twelve times in the *Revelation of the Magi*. This terminology is strongly connected with the language and theology of John's Gospel, where it appears more than twenty times.

63. Cf. Mt 2:11. This is the first of several instances where "his" accompanies the gifts that the Magi are to bring to Christ. The translation "his own" presupposes that the gifts in some way have always belonged to Christ, but why this should be so is not made explicit in the text. It is remarkable that the *Revelation of the Magi* nowhere clarifies precisely what these

the form of a star," rather than simply a star, is significant, since the star is actually the preexistent Christ.

58. The precise role and symbolism of this "pillar of light" in the narrative is unclear. Although the *Revelation of the Magi* mentions the pillar upon which the star sits ten times, these mentions are always during the sequence when the star appears, descends from heaven, and stands before the mouth of a cave (either in Shir or in Bethlehem). Thus, the pillar has no explicit role as a guide for the Magi during their journey; only the star is named at this point in the story. But it is difficult to understand the significance of this pillar without recourse to the Exodus narrative; indeed, the scribe responsible for the text wrote "pillar of cloud" instead of "pillar of light" at a point late in the narrative (27:4). This is the only time this phrase appears in the *Revelation of the Magi* (elsewhere it is "pillar of light"), so it may be no more than a transmission error, but at the very least, it demonstrates a possible (if unintentional) reference to Exodus.

59. Cf. 11:5–7 (and accompanying note at 11:5), 16:4.

60. Cf. Col 1:15.

61. Cf. Jn 4:14.

62. The phrase "who sent" (usually followed by "me") appears twelve times in the *Revelation of the Magi*. This terminology is strongly connected with the language and theology of John's Gospel, where it appears more than twenty times.

63. Cf. Mt 2:11. This is the first of several instances where "his" accompanies the gifts that the Magi are to bring to Christ. The translation "his own" presupposes that the gifts in some way have always belonged to Christ, but why this should be so is not made explicit in the text. It is remarkable that the *Revelation of the Magi* nowhere clarifies precisely what these gifts are, even if it might be expected that they are none other than the familiar gold, frankincense, and myrrh. This lack of interest in the gifts is rather odd and represents one of several departures of the *Revelation of the Magi* from common trends in ancient Christian exegesis of the Magi story. Other non-canonical traditions have the Magi giving the child a wide array of gifts; cf. the Irish *Leabhar Breac* infancy narrative 92.3 (an important witness to *Infancy Gospel X*), where they give a purple stone, a pearl, a garland, a linen sheet, a royal staff, and "other gifts, the like or equal of which has not been found on earth." In some traditions the Magi even receive a gift from Christ in turn: in the *Arabic Infancy Gospel* 8:1–6, Christ gives them a band of cloth that does not burn in fire; in the *Legend of Aphroditianus,* the Magi take back to Persia a picture of the child and mother painted by a servant; in a tale narrated to Marco Polo in Iran, a stone that produces holy fire.

64. The *Revelation of the Magi* also mentions the unsightliness of Christ's physical appearance at 14:5 and 28:2. Cf. the Apocryphal Acts of the Apostle Peter 20, which describes Christ as "beautiful and ugly, young and old." The *Revelation of the Magi* and the Acts of Peter share an emphasis on the ability of Christ to shift his form between that of luminous divine being and an unsightly and humble human being. It is possible that these passages refer back to Is 53:2.

65. Sic. It is unclear whether the passive participle of the verb "to kill" by itself is intended to have the valence of "mortal," if it foreshadows Christ's later death (cf. the "sign of the cross" in 4:8), or if some other meaning is intended for this difficult reading.

66. The commencing of the ritual on this date could suggest an allusion to the celebration of Christmas on December 25, the date established by the Roman church in 337. Some Eastern Christian communities—in particular, the

Jerusalem church—were resistant to this date until the fifth and sixth centuries, preferring the date of January 6. Yet the ritual's occurrence every month complicates this supposition, even if it is difficult to understand the significance of the twenty-fifth apart from the date of Christmas. Furthermore, the *Revelation of the Magi* has the Magi arrive in Jerusalem during the month of April, "the month of flowers" (17:1), and since they go to Bethlehem very soon after and witness the birth of Jesus in a cave, this would suggest the date of his birth sometime in April (though *birth* is not necessarily the best terminology for a transformation from star into a luminous child). In any case, the mention of the twenty-fifth of the month cannot be reliably used to argue for a post-Constantinian dating of the first-person section of the *Revelation of the Magi*.

125

67. This combination of trees occurring naturally within a single habitat is, from an ecological perspective, impossible, and thus is part of an idealized cultic landscape. The combination of a mountain, cave, spring, and sacred grove brings together some of the most characteristic features of sacred geography.

68. In ancient Jewish and Christian writings, especially pleasing smells often signify divinity and/or moral goodness. Syriac Christian writings are particularly noteworthy for their emphasis on this sometimes overlooked sense.

69. The *Revelation of the Magi* does not specify how much time has elapsed between the Magi's purification on the twenty-fifth of the month and their ascent of the mountain on the first day of the next month. If it follows a Roman calendar, the number of days in a given month would vary. Since this narrative is set in a semimythical country, however, it is very difficult to give precise durations for the different stages of the ritual.

70. Cf. 3:8.

71. This passage, which seems to indicate that some people rejected the teaching of the Magi, is very difficult to understand. The *Revelation of the Magi* never again discusses these dissenters (but cf. 28:1) and here indicates only that their rejection has to do with the practice of silent prayer espoused by the Magi (cf. note at 1:2). Silent prayer was rather uncommon in ancient religions and often viewed with some suspicion, but this is the only mention of it in the *Revelation of the Magi* that has a negative connotation.

72. The next four chapters are presented as an excerpt from the books of revelation produced by Seth and entrusted to the Magi. Though this extended flashback might appear to derail the progression of the plot by breaking away from the Magi, it explains the ultimate origins of the Magi's knowledge and details the first appearance of the star. In addition, since it occurs immediately after the description of the Magi's monthly ritual and immediately prior to the appearance of the star during their ritual, it provides the impression of the passage of some time between the initiation of the present generation of Magi by their fathers and the fulfillment of the ancient prophecy.

73. Cf. Gn 4:25.

74. Cf. 11:7 and 17:2, which indicate that the star was visible only to those who were deemed worthy to see it.

75. Cf. Mk 3:24.

76. Cf. Gn 2:21–22.

77. Cf. Gn 2:23.

78. Similar to 1:2 and 2:1 above, the phrasing of this sentence seems to imply a play on words between *time* and *stumbling block*. However, as with the apparent connection between *Magi* and *silence*, it is not at all clear what similarity exists between these two words.

79. Though the term *mysteries* is frequently used with reference to the central ritual of the Magi, it is not clear whether this statement is a directive only to Seth and only with reference to Eve, or whether it is understood to prohibit more broadly women's participation in the Magi's activities. While those who constitute the Magi's ranks are almost always gendered with masculine terms like *father* and *son*, the Magi also instruct their "families," of which women are certainly a part. Still, the handing down of tradition through the lineage of the Magi is predicated on transmission from father to son, with the son taking the father's place at his death, so the role of women is rather limited.

80. Cf. Gn 2:18.

81. Cf. Mk 1:11.

82. It is not clear precisely from where the ideas about Adam having priority before he was created and about the watchers loving him derive. This may be a distant echo of the tradition, found in the *Life of Adam and Eve* 14:1–3, that God instructed the angels to worship Adam.

83. Cf. Gn 4:10; Dn 4:35; Rom 9:20.

84. Cf. Gn 3:15.

85. Cf. Gn 3:14; Is 65:25; Mi 7:17; Rom 16:20.

86. It is not clear whether these individuals whose decline in the last days Adam predicts in 9:2–6 are the human race generally, the lineage of the Magi specifically, or perhaps some other group. But if the text means to imply that the Magi have fallen into apostasy, this is not suggested anywhere other than here.

87. The mention of blaspheming and "saying many things" stands in sharp contrast to the emphasis placed by the *Revelation of the Magi* on both the silent prayer of the Magi and the ineffability of the Father.

88. These criticisms of the veneration of heavenly bodies are especially interesting to find in a text so devoted to the Magi, since a chief concern of a number of ancient Christian exegetes regarding Mt 2:1–12 was the potential of this text to be read as demonstrating the efficacy of astrology. Beyond this passing comment, the overall depiction of the Magi in the *Revelation of the Magi* as less like a band of astrologers and more like a doomsday cult (i.e., waiting for one pivotal otherworldly event, not continually interpreting the sky to discern the present and foretell the future) may very well address from a different angle some of these same concerns. For examples of this uneasiness, see: Tertullian (*On Idolatry* 9), in which he asserts that the Magi left behind the magical practice of astrology after their visit to Bethlehem, deducing this from the information that they returned to their homeland "by another way"; John Chrysostom, (*Homilies on Matthew* 6.1), where he laments that some Christians infer the acceptability of astrological practices from Matthew's story.

89. Criticism of these sorts of acts of profligate living is quite widespread in ancient texts, so it is impossible to know whether these are directed at specific problems in a community or are simply stock phrases of moral exhortation. However, it is noteworthy that the *Revelation of the Magi*, unlike much early Syriac literature, does not have a strong ascetical agenda. The Magi do not engage in celibacy or other worlddenying practices, nor is such a lifestyle advocated by Judas Thomas at the end of the *Revelation of the Magi*, unlike his counterpart in Acts of Thomas.

90. Cf. Gn 3:5. The speaker of these words is, of course, the serpent.

91. Cf. Is 29:16, 45:9, 64:8; Jer 18:4–6.

92. Cf. Jn 13:16.

93. Cf. Gn 2:7.

94. This statement refers to the tradition of Christ descending into Hell in the time between his death and Resurrection, often called the "harrowing of Hell." The specific intention in the *Revelation of the Magi*, to redeem Adam, is also referenced in a number of ancient Christian texts, but other incidents (such as the binding of the devil) find mention as well. The tradition has its canonical origins in Eph 4:9 and 1 Pt 3:19–20, 4:6.

95. Cf. Gn 2:7.

96. Cf. Gn 4:1–2.

97. Cf. Gn 4:4.

98. Cf. Gn 4:10–12.

99. Cf. Gn 4:26; also 3:2 above.

100. It seems that 11:1–2 should not be read as a "real-time" description of the star's appearance, the account of which begins in 11:3. Instead, these two verses likely function as summary statements to indicate that the star appeared during this generation of Magi's time, and that the visions that they saw at the time of the star's coming were predicted by the books of revelation.

101. Several other early Christian texts describe the Magi's star as inordinately bright. The earliest such description is Ignatius of Antioch's *Epistle to the Ephesians* 19:2, where the star is brighter than all other stars, which form a circle around it. Somewhat later in the second century, in the *Protevangelium of James* 21:8, the Magi describe the star as being so bright that it makes all other stars disappear. There is no indication, however, in either of these texts that this celestial phenomenon is invisible to everyone except the Magi.

102. The month of Nisan is equivalent to April, though it is strange to have such a culturally specific reference in a text situated, for the most part, in a locale that is almost otherworldly. However, the phrase "in the days of Nisan" can also be translated idiomatically as "in springtime." In either case, see the note directly below.

103. I.e., "the moon is absorbed in the light of the sun." This statement is odd because it places the phenomenon of a faint daytime moon at a specific time of the year—namely, Nisan/ April (or possibly springtime). However, as is well known, the daytime moon is visible throughout the entire year, and not simply in April. The analogy itself—that the star is so bright that it makes the sun appear as faint as the daytime moon normally does—is quite clear, creative, and vivid, even if the reference to April is difficult to understand.

104. The phrase "the sons of our mysteries" (as opposed to "our sons" at 5:1) seems to indicate, along with 5:9 and 5:11, that the order of the Magi does not perpetuate strictly through biological succession (as 5:10 might imply) but is open to "converts."

105. The tradition that the star of the Magi was visible only to them is a definite minority position in ancient Christian exegesis. It is, however, one of several striking agreements between the *Revelation of the Magi* and *Infancy Gospel X*. Because these two texts agree on what is such an unusual interpretation of the Star of Bethlehem, it is very likely that there is some sort of literary relationship between them.

106. Cf. Jn 1:51; Gn 28:12.

107. Cf. 4:2 and corresponding note.

108. Cf. 20:1.

109. Cf. 4:8. Latin and Irish witnesses to *Infancy Gospel X* also describe the birth of Christ as a mass of light that gradually dissipates until it assumes the form of an infant.

110. Cf. Lk 24:36; Jn 20:19, 21, 26.

111. Cf. 19:1, 21:2, 25:1, 31:1.

112. Cf. Jn 1:14.

113. Cf. Jn 3:16.

114. Cf. Jn 19:30.

115. Cf. Phil 2:8.

116. Cf. Gal 4:4.

117. Cf. Rom 1:20, 2:1.

118. This idea that Christ can be both in the presence of the Father and on earth at the same time may be related to a variant reading in Jn 3:13, which states that the Son of Man, who has ascended into and descended from heaven, is (currently) in heaven. Regardless of the origin of the idea, however, the *Revelation of the Magi* is evidently very invested in the ability of Christ to appear in multiple locations and forms simultaneously.

119. Cf. Col 3:11; Gospel of Thomas 77.

120. This sentence contains an intriguing theological concept: that Christ is the underlying reality of all systems of religious belief in the world. Although other early Christian writings admit the possibility of revelation through non-Christian channels (e.g., Acts 14:15–17, 17:22–31), the *Revelation of the Magi* demonstrates a novel "theology of world religions," the precise form of which is found nowhere else, to my knowledge, in ancient Christian sources.

121. Cf. Ez 3:9.

122. Cf. Gospel of Philip 57:28–58:10.

123. The idea that those involved in the killing of Christ have come to an evil end appears in numerous early Christian writings (e.g., 1 Thes 2:15; Mt 27:25).

124. The final phrase of this sentence is rather difficult to understand. It may mean that there were letters that the Magi were to open only at the time of the star's coming, giving specific instructions for the gifts to be brought. However, the more likely sense is that the gifts, whatever they were, were housed in some kind of sealed container(s), here called "letters." This is the probable meaning, based upon the statement in 18:7 that the Magi had brought their treasures to Bethlehem "sealed."

125. The series of statements that follow demonstrate Christ's polymorphous ability, a tradition that appears in a number of other ancient Christian texts. This concept seems to derive from the account of Jesus's transfiguration (Mk 9:2–8) and from the Resurrection appearance stories, but it undergoes considerable development in the second and third centuries, where it appears in the Acts of John 88–94, the Acts of Thomas 143, and the Acts of Peter 20–21. In some traditions about the Magi, including the *Armenian Infancy Gospel* and a legend told to Marco Polo in Iran in the twelfth century, Jesus appeared to each of the three Magi in correspondence to their ages: as young, middle-aged, and old. In another impressive parallel to the *Revelation of the Magi,* the best Latin witness of *Infancy Gospel X* has the infant Jesus change his form as the shepherds are viewing. A unique aspect of the polymorphic vision in the *Revelation of the Magi,* not seen in other texts, is that its individual pieces in sequence tell the story of Christ's birth, growth, and death, culminating with his descent into Sheol and his heavenly ascent. A polymorphic appearance of Christ also occurs later in the *Revelation of the Magi,* this time for the inhabitants of Shir after they have eaten of the food brought back by the Magi (28:1–3).

126. Regarding Christ's ugliness, see note at 4:8.

127. Cf. Jn 1:29.

128. Cf. 10:4 and corresponding note.

129. Cf. 12:3; Ps 24:7.

130. Cf. Ps 91:12.

131. Cf. Jn 14:16, 14:26, 15:26, 16:7; 1 Jn 2:1.

132. Cf. Mt 13:17; Lk 10:24.

133. Cf. Acts 9:3, 22:6, 26:13.

134. Cf. Mt 11:27; Lk 10:22.

135. Cf. Jn 1:18, 10:38. This verse of the *Revelation of the Magi* uses several terms—*singleness, thought, voice*—that are relatively rare in early Christian literature and have their closest parallels in the Gnostic Christian writings from Nag Hammadi (see also the frequent references to "error" at 13:3, 13:5, 14:8, 17:9, 18:1, 21:9, 21:10, 30:4, 32:2). Some scholars have considered the *Revelation of the Magi* to be a "Gnostic" text; however, despite this strange terminology, the *Revelation of the Magi* lacks any traces of the most common doctrines found in the Nag Hammadi literature, such as a negative evaluation of the material world or an evil creator (cf. 21:9).

136. Cf. Jn 1:3.

137. Cf. Rom 8:38–39; Col 1:16.

138. Cf. 2:2.

139. Cf. Mk 1:11, 9:7.

140. Cf. 1:5.

141. Cf. Col 1:15.

142. Cf. Jn 1:14, 1:18, 3:16, 3:18; 1 Jn 4:9.

143. Cf. Jn 3:19.

144. In the Syriac tradition, the terminology of "putting on a body" is a very typical description of the Incarnation.

145. Cf. Mk 16:17.

146. Cf. Jn 14:6.

147. Cf. Jn 10:9.

148. Cf. Phil 2:9.

149. Cf. Jn 6:35, 48, 51. Also note that the pronoun *me* provides the first indication of who is speaking this discourse: the Father himself, as will become completely clear with the final words of the passage in 15:10.

150. Cf. Mk 4:14.

151. Cf. Jn 10:11.

152. Cf. Heb 4:14.

153. Cf. Jn 6:55.

154. Cf. Jn 15:1, 5.

155. The use of *encampment* here and at several places in the rest of the narrative is peculiar, since it does not suggest a relatively small group of travelers. It is a word used in the New Testament almost exclusively for large assemblies of people (e.g., Acts 21:34; Heb 11:34, 13:11). Because of this typical usage, this terminology in the *Revelation of the Magi* may reflect a more archaic belief that the group of the Magi numbered more than twelve (cf. the list of names in 2:3, which is possibly an independent accretion grafted onto the *Revelation of the Magi*). If this is indeed the case, then this would be another similarity between the *Revelation of the Magi* and *Infancy Gospel X*, whose witnesses all portray the Magi as a large group of people.

156. The ambiguity of this verb does not specify whether the group of the Magi is being upheld in the sense of "being sustained" or actually "carried" off the ground. Evidence for both interpretations appears in 16:6, as the Magi are relieved of their fatigue and cross rivers by foot.

157. Cf. Is 60:19; Rv 21:23, 22:5.

158. A reference to the lack of fatigue experienced by the Magi also occurs in an Irish witness to *Infancy Gospel X*. It is also possible that this passage from the *Revelation of the Magi* alludes to Is 40:31.

159. I.e., the star.

160. Cf. 26:5, 27:9. This food that is generated by the star will later figure prominently in the conversion of the people of Shir, since it produces visions of Christ for those who eat it (28:1–4). While the multiplication of food has some parallels in early Christian literature (cf. Mk 6:32–44, 8:10; Jn 6:5–13; *Infancy Gospel of Thomas* 12), the ability of food to facilitate visionary experience is far more unusual. Several similar concepts are the eating of a scroll as a sign of prophetic commission in Ez 2:8–3:3 and Rv 10:8–10 and the eating of a heavenly honeycomb by Aseneth as a kind of proto-Eucharist in *Joseph and Aseneth* 16; but even in these cases, there is no indication that what is ingested produces a visionary experience.

161. Cf. Is 40:4.

162. Cf. Gn 3:15; Ps 91:13; Lk 10:19; Rom 16:20.

163. I.e., in April (Nisan; cf. 11:6). Clement of Alexandria also knows of Christians who state that Jesus was born in April (24–25 Pharmuti, equivalent to April 20–21); see *Miscellanies* 1.21. The information that the Magi arrived in "the month of flowers" also appears in Theodore bar Konai (*Mimra* 7.17). Because of such similar language, it is very likely that Theodore was acquainted with the *Revelation of the Magi*. Moreover, Theodore was writing in central Arabia at roughly the same time that the *Chronicle of Zuqnin* was produced, which indicates that the *Revelation of the Magi* was in fairly wide circulation at the end of the eighth century.

164. Cf. Mt 2:3.

165. This statement by the inhabitants of Jerusalem and the

explanatory comments of the Magi that follow are noteworthy on several levels. First of all, there is again a remarkable
parallel with *Infancy Gospel X*, where *Joseph* (not the inhabitants of Jerusalem) regards the Magi as astrologers because
they are constantly looking up at the sky. More precisely, in
both texts the Magi are watching their guiding star, which
neither the inhabitants of Jerusalem nor Joseph is able to see
(cf. 11:7). Beyond this, however, there is a more problematic
issue. The use of the term *Magianism* occurs only here in the
Revelation of the Magi; their religious system is elsewhere
called *mysteries, custom,* or *faith.* Moreover, this is also the
only instance of the word *Magi* within the first-person-plural
narration that makes up the bulk of the document, and its
connotation is apparently negative. Because the inhabitants of
Jerusalem refer to the actions of the visitors as "Magianism,"
do not understand the mysteries of these visitors, and reckon
these visitors to be "Magi," the entire implication of this passage is that these visitors are not who the inhabitants of Jerusalem think they are, and are *not* Magi—a difficult conclusion
given that the central figures of the narrative are obviously
the Magi. Perhaps a solution lies in the earlier statements that
the Magi are called by this name because of their silent prayer
(1:2, 2:1), which may be intended in part to differentiate these
figures from the more common connotation of Magi as astrologers.

166. Cf. 15:7 and accompanying note.

167. Cf. 13:10 and corresponding note.

168. Cf. Mt 2:4.

169. Cf. Mt 2:10.

170. The statement that the scribes did not believe that which
was written in their sacred writings, when coupled with the
Magi's reliance on their own books of prophecy, sharply con-

trasts the two groups and goes beyond the implicit critique already present in Matthew.

171. Perhaps this is an allusion to Gn 1:3.

172. It is possible to understand this sentence as an indictment of the Jewish people since the time of Herod: "They are (still) dwelling in darkness (as they have done) from the days of Herod. . . ."

173. Cf. Mt 2:8.

174. Cf. Mt 2:12.

175. Cf. Jn 8:12, 9:5.

176. The Syriac term used here can also mean a court, a space enclosed by a fence, or a sheepfold. I have chosen the translation "homestead" because of the immediate appearance of Mary and Joseph as the Magi are leaving the cave (22:2), an indication that they do not live far away from the cave.

177. Although in Mt 2:11 the Magi visit the infant Jesus in his parents' house, here the *Revelation of the Magi* places the birth in a cave, a locale mentioned in several other ancient sources. While Lk 2:7 has Jesus laid in a "manger" because there was no room in the "inn," many scholars believe that this verse is describing a very rudimentary shelter for travelers, not the sort of inn found, for example, in Luke's parable of the Good Samaritan (cf. Lk 10:34, which uses a different Greek word for "inn"). It is therefore possible that the primitive structure that Luke describes evolved into the belief that Jesus was born in a cave. The cave tradition also appears in the *Protevangelium of James* 18.1; the Syriac *Testament of Adam* 3:6; Justin Martyr *Dialogue with Trypho* 78; and a number of other early Christian writers.

178. The sequence of events in 18:3–5 is practically identical to the initial manifestation of the star to the Magi atop the Mountain of Victories.

179. This is the first of several statements, which occur at various places in the narrative, indicating that the mysteries of the Magi have been accomplished or fulfilled (cf. 19:2, 21:4, 24:2, 31:1).

180. Cf. 11:4.

181. Cf. 12:3.

182. Cf. 12:4.

183. Cf. 12:5.

184. This is the only reference in the first-person-plural section of the *Revelation of the Magi* that implies that the Magi are kings. Cf. 1:2, 2:3–5.

185. Cf. Mt 6:13, though this part of the Lord's Prayer does not appear in the earliest Greek manuscripts.

186. Cf. Rom 14:11; Phil 2:10.

187. Cf. Mt 19:28–29; Mk 10:30; Lk 18:29–30.

188. Cf. 13:1, 21:1, 25:1, 31:1.

189. How the fathers of the Magi are able to see the light of the star is not clear, since 5:10 implies that their sons would be initiated into the Magi's mysteries only when their fathers had died; perhaps the text means only that they were *worthy* to see it, even if it did not appear in their lifetimes.

190. Cf. Mt 28:20.

191. Cf. the appearance of Judas Thomas in 29:1, but there is never any indication in the final portion of the *Revelation of the Magi* that more than one disciple preaches in the homeland of the Magi.

192. Cf. Jn 17:5.

193. Cf. 13:9.

194. Cf. Mk 15:33.

195. Cf. Mt 27:51–52. This prediction of events, which in the New Testament occurs in conjunction with the death of Jesus, is problematic in that it is never again mentioned in the *Revelation of the Magi*. If the Judas Thomas episode is judged to be an interpolation, then it is possible that its insertion may have obliterated the fulfillment of this prophecy.

196. Cf. Mk 14:62, 16:19; Acts 7:55–56.

197. Cf. 12:4.

198. The Latin and Irish witnesses to *Infancy Gospel X* also state that the Christ child received praise from invisible heavenly beings at the moment of his birth.

199. Cf. Jn 1:3.

200. Cf. 2 Cor 1:20.

201. Cf. Col 1:16.

202. Cf. 2:2.

203. The Magi falling on the ground like dead men in 21:1 and the child putting his right hand on them in 21:2 very strongly resemble Rv 1:17.

204. Cf. 13:1, 19:1, 25:1, 31:1.

205. It is not clear what these "great things" to come are. It is possible that this refers back to the prophecy spoken by the child in 19:7–9 regarding the events at his death and his ascension to heaven.

206. I.e., Shir, where the light of the star first appeared.

207. Cf. 29:5.

208. Cf. 27:10.

209. Cf. Col 1:15.

210. Cf. 1 Cor 1:24.

211. Cf. Jn 10:38; 14:11.

212. Cf. 13:10; Jn 5:46.

213. Cf. Gospel of Thomas 50.

214. Cf. Gospel of Thomas 12.

215. Cf. 30:5–6, 31:1. It is important to note that the Holy Spirit is feminine in gender here, as evidenced by the feminine form of the adjective *holy.* This usage, found in the second-century *Odes of Solomon* and the fourth-century writings of Ephrem and Aphrahat, indicates a probable date earlier than the fifth century for the *Revelation of the Magi,* since Syriac writers after this time generally understand the Holy Spirit as a masculine entity.

216. This statement about infants lacking any blemishes of sin is intriguing, since it disagrees markedly with the Augustinian conception of original sin, wherein infants, like all of humanity, share Adam's guilt (*On Merit and the Forgiveness of Sin, and the Baptism of Infants* 1.9.24). The assertion that infants lack sin occurs in a number of Greek Christian writers (cf. Aristides *Apology* 15, Syriac recension; Clement of Alexandria *Miscellanies* 4.25.160; Gregory of Nyssa *On Infants' Early Deaths*, passim).

217. I.e., the Father of majesty.

218. Cf. 32:2.

219. Cf. Rv 5:13.

220. The appearance of Mary and Joseph at this point in the narrative is quite abrupt, as the *Revelation of the Magi* does not mention them earlier. It is not clear whether they "went out" of the cave or the village of Bethlehem with the Magi. This episode is also remarkable for the way in which it uses the misunderstanding of Mary and Joseph as the first occasion for the Magi to act as witnesses for Christ by proclaiming his true omnipresent nature. In *Infancy Gospel X*, it is also the Magi who convey to Joseph and his son Simeon the significance of Christ's birth.

221. The statement "the offspring of the voice of virgin hearing" (cf. also 24:3) seems to demonstrate a familiarity with the ancient Christian doctrine that Mary's conception happened through auditory channels—i.e., through her ear. Although the doctrine becomes especially popular in the mid-fifth century and beyond, traces of it appear as early as the second-century *Protevangelium of James*. In its annunciation narrative, Gabriel tells Mary that she will conceive from God's word (*Protevangelium of James* 11:5).

222. Cf. 28:2.

223. Cf. 4:8, 13:1.

224. Cf. Mk 14:9.

225. Cf. Mt 2:11.

226. Cf. Ascension of Isaiah 11:8–9.

227. Cf. Lk 1:42.

228. The beginning section of this sentence is problematic, since it would be expected that the child is no longer in Mary's womb. This statement may suggest that Christ is always with Mary, as he is always with the Magi—an indication of Christ's omnipresence.

229. I.e., "by the majesty of the Father of all."

230. This statement of the Magi to Mary strongly reflects the interest in universal salvation through the polymorphism and omnipresence of Christ (cf. 13:10 and corresponding note).

231. It is unclear whether the Magi have accompanied Mary and Joseph to their house, since they are not mentioned again until 26:1. If they have not, then chapters 24 and 25 would be a rather jarring departure from the first-person narration that pervades the majority of the *Revelation of the Magi*. Since the location of the Bethlehem cave is described as a "homestead" (cf. 18:2 and corresponding note), this may indicate that there is very little space between the cave and the house of Mary and Joseph.

232. Instances of Jesus laughing in ancient Christian texts are quite rare; however, the recently published *Gospel of Judas* has Jesus laugh on several occasions at the misunderstandings of his disciples. *Infancy Gospel X* also depicts the newborn Jesus as laughing.

233. Cf. 22:2 and corresponding note.

234. Mary's misunderstanding here is intriguing: she apparently thought that the gifts brought by the Magi were a sort of bribe that they offered to the divine child so that he would accompany them.

235. Cf. 13:1, 19:1, 21:2, 31:1.

236. Cf. 23:1; Lk 1:42.

237. Cf. Lk 1:48

238. Cf. Gn 3:24; Lk 2:35. In linking the instrument that guarded the Garden of Eden with that which is said to pierce Mary's heart, the *Revelation of the Magi* resembles to a certain degree an interpretation found in several Syriac texts, wherein the spear that pierces Christ's side in Jn 19:34 reverses the sword in Genesis.

239. Cf. Col 3:11; Gospel of Thomas 77.

240. I.e., the sun.

241. It is not clear who "all your believers" are, with whom the Magi have been witnesses to the star. The only other people who have seen the star are Mary and Joseph; however, it may refer to the statements made by Christ and the Magi that he has adherents in every land (13:10; 17:5).

242. Cf. 16:5, 27:9.

243. Cf. 14:3.

244. Cf. 16:4 and accompanying note.

245. This is the first instance in the *Revelation of the Magi* of indirect discourse being used to summarize a speech, as opposed to the regular pattern of directly quoting lengthy speeches. The only other such occurrences of this are in 29:3–4, where the Magi tell the Apostle Thomas about their journey and Thomas in turn relates to them his experiences with the earthly Jesus. Note also that by 27:9, the indirect discourse has evidently switched to direct speech, as indicated by the presence of "you." Because of this shift back and forth between indirect and direct speech and also the parallels of this section with the Thomas material, it is likely that this section reveals editorial tampering designed to integrate the first-person testimony of the Magi with the new third-person ending featuring the Apostle Thomas.

246. Sic. Cf. note at 12:3.

247. It is unclear precisely what the meaning of this sentence is.

248. Cf. 13:10.

249. Cf. note at 4:7.

250. Cf. 13:10.

251. This phrase may be meant as a critique of Judaism, since "the prophets" are also mentioned in 13:10.

252. Cf. 26:1.

253. Cf. 16:5, 26:5.

254. Cf. note at 27:3.

255. Cf. 21:6.

256. Cf. Jn 1:9.

257. Cf. 23:4.

258. Cf. 5:11 for the only other indication that not all the people of Shir choose to participate in the mysteries of the Magi.

259. The visions of the people of Shir in 28:1–3 are related in the same basic form as those experienced by the Magi in 14:4–8. However, two features distinguish these visions from those of the Magi. First, these visions are facilitated simply by the eating of food, while those of the Magi resulted from the epiphany of Christ in the Cave of Treasures. Second, the visions of the Magi followed in sequence the order of events in Christ's life, whereas here the order is less secure and the account of Christ's life less complete.

260. Cf. 22:3.

261. Cf. 11:6.

262. Cf. 4:8 and accompanying note.

263. Cf. Jn 1:29, 36; Rv 5:6.

264. Although the phrase "tree of life" appears in 6:2, here another Syriac word is used for "tree" instead. While this Syriac word can also designate Eden's Tree of Life (as in Rv 22:2), in a number of New Testament texts it refers to the cross (cf. Acts 5:30; Gal 3:13).

265. Cf. Acts 2:1.

266. Cf. note at 28:6.

Notes

267. Cf. 1:2. It is at this point that, for the first time since 2:6 or 3:6 (unless chapters 24 and 25 are an exception; see the note at 24:1), the narration is no longer in the first-person plural, but in the third person. This transition may have happened earlier, at 28:1, but the description of the Magi in the third person demonstrates unambiguously that they are no longer the narrators of the *Revelation of the Magi*.

268. I.e., the nobles, the poor, the women, and the children of Shir.

269. I.e., the Magi.

270. Cf. Acts 17:19.

271. This is the first use in the *Revelation of the Magi* of the title "Our Lord Jesus Christ," a very widespread designation in Christian piety; its presence strongly suggests that a later Syriac writer tampered with the text. The portion of the text narrated by the Magi themselves (the overwhelming bulk of the *Revelation of the Magi*) never uses the name "Jesus" or "Christ" to describe the being whom the Magi encounter. In contrast, this terminology is used very frequently in the short Apostle Thomas section, where some combination of these designations occurs eighteen times. The sudden preference for this familiar Christian terminology is one of the strongest arguments (cf. also the switch from first-person to third-person narration in 28:4) in favor of the theory that the Apostle Thomas section is a later addition to the *Revelation of the Magi*. It is possible that whoever added the Apostle Thomas material was troubled by the fact that the first-person Magi narrative never explicitly integrates the Magi into the wider Christian Church.

272. Cf. Acts 2:47.

273. Judas Thomas is the same as the apostle known simply as "Thomas" in the Synoptic Gospels (cf. Mk 3:18; Mt 10:3; Lk

6:15; also Acts 1:13) and as "Thomas who was called Didymus" in John's Gospel (11:16, 20:24, 21:2). The Greek nickname "Didymus" means "twin," and the Syriac name "Thomas" is also related to the Aramaic word for "twin." The name "Judas Thomas" is found in two texts from Nag Hammadi (the *Gospel of Thomas* and the *Book of Thomas the Contender*), as well as in the Acts of Thomas. It appears that Judas Thomas was the chief apostolic figure in ancient Syriac-speaking Christianity, particularly in the environs of Edessa. In the Acts of Thomas, Judas Thomas is commissioned to preach the gospel in India, where he is eventually martyred, but the *Revelation of the Magi* either ignores or is not aware of this tradition in favor of placing him in the farthest reaches of the East. There are some later references to a mission of the Apostle Thomas in China, and it is possible that these traditions ultimately go back to the *Revelation of the Magi*.

274. Cf. 21:5.

275. Cf. Acts 9:19.

276. Cf. 27:3 and accompanying note.

277. Though the text changed to narration in the third person at 28:4, here it curiously breaks into the first-person plural yet again with "we are not able to narrate," "appearing to us," and "we were amazed." However, the "we" in this case is certainly not the Magi, but instead the disciples of Christ, whose experience with the polymorphic Christ the Apostle Thomas is describing.

278. The mention of doubt in connection with Thomas may allude to Jn 20:24–29.

279. Cf. 21:5. Although in the earlier passage it was unclear precisely what the "seal" was, here it is obviously Christian baptism—terminology perhaps derived from Eph 1:13, 4:30.

280. The order represented here of anointing with oil first, baptism second (cf. 31:1), is a practice particular to Syriac Christianity and is attested in other ancient sources.

281. The prayer/hymn spoken here by the Apostle Thomas is unattested in any other ancient sources, but it appears to be quite archaic because of vocabulary not seen elsewhere in the *Revelation of the Magi* ("athletes," "contest," "partner of the firstborn," etc.). These elements suggest that the prayer had an origin separate from the other sections of the *Revelation of the Magi*, most likely in a liturgical context. This hymn, particularly its invocations to "come" (cf. 30:7), finds its closest parallel in the prayers scattered throughout the Acts of Thomas. The similarity of this prayer to those of the Acts of Thomas and the failure to mention the Apostle Thomas's well-known journey to India suggest that the Apostle Thomas section originated quite early in Syriac Christianity, even if it is only a secondary addition to the original *Revelation of the Magi*.

147

282. I.e., the oil.

283. Cf. Mt 28:19.

284. Cf. 13:1,19:1, 21:2, 25:1.

285. Cf. 21:1.

286. Cf. Phil 2:19.

287. I.e., God the Father. This speech of the Apostle Thomas is ambiguous in whether or not it believes that Christ suffered. 31:6 states that Christ "endured" everything that the crucifiers did to him, but also that he was "exalted above all sufferings" and "a kinsperson of that one who does not suffer." However, 31:7 again states that Christ "endured everything and . . . suffered everything," which seems, on its face, to be a clear belief in the suffering of Christ.

288. Cf. Acts 2:47.

289. Cf. Mt 28:19.

290. It is unclear whether the Apostle Thomas joins the Magi in their preaching, since 32:1–2 never states specifically who "they" are. For the *Opus Imperfectum in Matthaeum,* it seems that the Magi follow Thomas in a subservient role. The reference to the Holy Spirit being poured out could suggest that it is the Magi alone who preach, since they have just received it in their baptism, but this statement in no way definitively excludes Thomas.

291. Cf. 21:11.

292. This is the first and only reference to a final judgment of fire that appears in the *Revelation of the Magi,* and it is not clear from whom the Magi received this information. The concept of a fiery end of the world exists in a number of ancient sources (cf. 2 Pt 3:7, 10). One related text is the reference of Josephus (*Antiquities* 1.68–69) to the descendants of Seth who live in the land of Seiris and transmitted a revelation from Adam that two catastrophes, one of water and one of fire, would overtake the earth.

293. The use of *my* here is strange, if it is assumed that the Magi (and the Apostle Thomas?) are preaching together. It may indicate that the preachers are working separately in different parts of the land of Shir, but this is never stated explicitly.

294. Cf. 1:1 and corresponding note. This final verse almost certainly derives from the eighth-century composer of the *Chronicle of Zuqnin* and not from the copy of the *Revelation of the Magi* that he used.

295. Thomas Aquinas's remarks on the Magi legend of the *Opus Imperfectum* appear in the third part of his *Summa,* question 36, article 5.

Notes

296. It is not clear to me whether Calancha supposed, like Columbus, that the American continent was part of Asia, or whether he correctly recognized that it was a separate landmass. Explorers of the New World were remarkably adept at making their discoveries "fit" the biblical descriptions of the world.

297. The "contentious house" is the house of Israel, as described in Ez 3:9.

ᗡNCIENT SOURCES

Budge, E. A. W. *The Book of the Cave of Treasures.* London: Religious Tract Society, 1927. A Syriac retelling of biblical history from Adam to Christ. It has its own "Cave of Treasures" but otherwise shows no obvious links to the *Revelation of the Magi.*

Chabot, J.-B. *Chronicon anonymum Pseudo-Dionysianum vulgo dictum, I. Corpus Scriptorum Christianorum Orientalium, Scriptores Syri, 3:1.* Paris: E Typographeo Reipublicae, 1927. The most recent critical edition of the *Chronicle of Zuqnin.* It includes the Syriac text and a Latin translation of the *Revelation of the Magi.*

James, M. R. *Latin Infancy Gospels.* Cambridge: Cambridge Univ. Press, 1927. Latin texts of two major witnesses to *Infancy Gospel X.* It includes an English translation of the Magi episode.

McNamara, M., et al. *Apocrypha Hiberniae I: Evangelia Infantiae.* Corpus Christianorum Series Apocryphorum 13–14. 2 vols. Turnhout: Brepols, 2001. Old Irish text and English translation of another major witness to *Infancy Gospel X.*

Migne, J.-P. "Liber apocryphus nomine Seth." Columns 637–638 in volume 56 of *Patrologia Graeca.* 162 volumes.

Paris: Imprimerie Catholique, 1857–86. A very important secondary witness to the *Revelation of the Magi;* a summary of the narrative from the fifth-century *Opus Imperfectum in Matthaeum.*

Roberts, A., and J. Donaldson. "The Arabic Gospel of the Infancy of Our Savior." In *The Ante-Nicene Fathers,* 8: 405–15. 10 vols. 1885–87. Reprint, Peabody, MA: Hendrickson, 1994. Apocryphal Infancy Gospel in which the Magi learn about Christ's birth through a prophecy of Zoroaster.

————. "Narrative of Events Happening in Persia on the Birth of Christ." In *The Ante-Nicene Fathers,* 6:128–30. 10 vols. 1885–87. Reprint, Peabody, MA: Hendrickson, 1994. An apocryphal writing in which the Magi figure heavily; also known as the *Legend of Aphroditianus.*

Ryan, W. G. *Jacobus de Voragine, The Golden Legend: Readings on the Saints.* 2 vols. Princeton, NJ: Princeton Univ. Press, 1993. An English translation of a medieval collection of Christian legends. It utilizes the *Opus Imperfectum in Matthaeum* for its information on the Magi.

Tullberg, O. F. *Dionysii Telmahharensis Chronici liber primus. Textum e codice ms. Syriaco Bibliothecae Vaticanae.* Uppsala: Regiae Academiae Typographi, 1850. First critical edition of the Syriac text of the *Chronicle of Zuqnin.*

Wright, W. "Eusebius of Caesarea on the Star." *Journal of Sacred Literature and Biblical Record* 9 (1866): 117–136; 10 (1867): 150–164. Another Syriac legend of the Magi in which they expect the coming of the star, though here it is Balaam and not Seth who is the originator of the prophecy.

Bibliography

MODERN SOURCES

Allison, D. C. "The Magi's Angel (2:2, 9–10)." In *Studies in Matthew: Interpretation Past and Present*, 17–41. Grand Rapids, MI: Baker, 2005. Overview of ancient Christian understandings of the Star of Bethlehem.

Boyce, M., and F. Grenet. *Zoroastrianism Under Macedonian and Roman Rule*. Vol. 3 of *A History of Zoroastrianism*. Leiden: E. J. Brill, 1991. Discusses the *Revelation of the Magi* and other early Christian interpretations of the Magi story.

Brock, S. P. "An Archaic Syriac Prayer over Baptismal Oil." In *Studia Patristica: Papers Presented at the Fourteenth International Congress on Patristic Studies Held in Oxford 2003*, edited by F. Young, M. Edwards, and P. Parvis, 3–12. Leuven: Peeters, 2006. Examines the Apostle Thomas's baptismal prayer in the *Revelation of the Magi*, and concludes (independently of my own research) that it dates to the time of the *Acts of Thomas*.

Brown, R. E. *The Birth of the Messiah: A Commentary on the Infancy Narratives in the Gospels of Matthew and Luke*. 2nd ed. New York: Doubleday, 1993. The premier scholarly commentary on the canonical infancy narratives.

Denzey, N. F. "A New Star on the Horizon: Astral Christologies and Stellar Debates in Early Christian Discourse." In *Prayer, Magic, and the Stars in the Ancient and Late Antique World*, edited by S. Noegel, J. Walker, and B. Wheeler, 207–21. University Park: Pennsylvania State Univ. Press, 2003. Examines the function of the Star of Bethlehem in early Christian debates about astrology.

Bibliography

Duchesne-Guillemin, J. "The Wise Men from the East in the Western Tradition." In *Papers in Honour of Professor Mary Boyce,* edited by J. Duchesne-Guillemin and P. Lecoq, 1:149–57. 2 vols. Leiden: Brill, 1985. Interprets the *Adoration of the Magi* from the Cloisters Museum (see page 51).

Foster, P. "Polymorphic Christology: Its Origins and Development in Early Christianity." *Journal of Theological Studies* 58 (2007): 66–99. An overview of early Christian texts that present Christ as capable of appearing in multiple forms.

Hultgard, A. "The Magi and the Star: The Persian Background in Texts and Iconography." In *"Being Religious and Living Through the Eyes": Studies in Religious Iconography and Iconology,* edited by P. Schalk and M. Stausberg, 215–25. Uppsala: Uppsala Univ. Library, 1998. Summarizes scholarly research on the *Revelation of the Magi* that argues for or against an Iranian origin of the text.

Kaestli, J.-D. "Recherches nouvelles sur les 'Évangiles latins de l'enfance' de M. R. James et sur un récit apocryphe mal connu de la naissance de Jésus." *Études Théologiques et Religieuses* 72 (1997): 219–233. Argues that *Infancy Gospel X* is possibly the oldest apocryphal Infancy Gospel, even older than the *Protevangelium of James.*

Kehl, A. "Der Stern der Magier: Zu §94 des lateinischen Kindheitsevangeliums der Arundel-Handschrift." *Jahrbuch für Antike und Christentum* 18 (1975): 69–80. Compares the *Revelation of the Magi* to the Magi episode from a Latin witness to *Infancy Gospel X.*

Kehrer, H. *Die Heiligen Drei Könige in Literatur und Kunst.* 2 vols. Leipzig: E. A. Seemann, 1908. Foundational study of the iconography of the Magi, from early through medieval Christianity.

Bibliography

Landau, B. C. "'One Drop of Salvation from the House of Majesty': Universal Revelation, Human Mission, and Mythical Geography in the Syriac *Revelation of the Magi.*" In *Proceedings of Late Antique Crossroads in the Levant Research Colloquium*, edited by E. B. Aitken and J. M. Fossey. Leiden: E. J. Brill, forthcoming. Examines the unusual beliefs of the *Revelation of the Magi* concerning Christology, revelation, and mission.

————. "The *Revelation of the Magi* in the *Chronicle of Zuqnin.*" *Apocrypha* 19 (2008): 182–201. Introduces the major scholarly issues regarding the *Revelation of the Magi.*

————. *The Sages and the Star-Child: An Introduction to the* Revelation of the Magi, *An Ancient Christian Apocryphon*. Th.D diss., Harvard Divinity School, 2008. First translation and major scholarly study of the *Revelation of the Magi* in English. Accessible online at http://ou.academia.edu/BrentLandau/Papers.

————. "The Unknown Apostle: A Pauline Agraphon in Clement of Alexandria's *Stromateis.*" *Annali di Storia dell'Esegesis* 25 (2008): 117–27. Interpretation of a "quotation" of the Apostle Paul asserting pagan foreknowledge of Christ's coming.

Luz, U. *Matthew 1–7. Hermeneia: A Critical and Historical Commentary on the Bible*. Edited by H. Koester. Translated by J. E. Crouch. Minneapolis: Fortress Press, 2007. The most recent major commentary on Matthew, emphasizing the history of interpretation of the Magi story.

Monneret de Villard, U. *Le leggende orientali sui Magi evangelici*. Studi e Testi 163. Vatican City: Biblioteca Apostolica Vaticana, 1952. A thorough overview of eastern Christian legends about the Magi. It includes an Italian translation and analysis of the *Revelation of the Magi.*

Reed, A. Y. "Beyond the Land of Nod: Syriac Images of Asia and the Historiography of the West." *History of Religions* 49 (2009): 48–87. Discusses the *Revelation of the Magi* as one of several examples of Syriac Christian imaginings of China.

Reinick, G. J. "Das Land 'Seiris' (Šir) und das Volk der Serer in jüdischen und christlichen Traditionen." *Journal for the Study of Judaism* 6 (1975): 72–85. Studies ancient Greek, Roman, Jewish, and Christian beliefs about the land of Shir and its inhabitants.

Screech, M. A. "The Magi and the Star (Matthew, 2)." In *Histoire de l'exégèse au XVIᵉ siècle*, edited by O. Fatio and P. Fraenkel, 385–409. Geneva: Droz, 1978. Examines the influence of the *Opus Imperfectum in Matthaeum* on medieval and Renaissance views of the Magi.

Trexler, R. C. *The Journey of the Magi: Meanings in History of a Christian Story*. Princeton, NJ: Princeton Univ. Press, 1997. An overview of the history of interpretation of Magi story, emphasizing its political dimensions.

Tubach, J. "Der Apostel Thomas in China: Die Herkunft einer Tradition." *Zeitschrift für Kirchengeschichte* 108 (1997): 58–74. Examines traditions that the Apostle Thomas visited China as a missionary.

Widengren, G. *Iranisch-semitische Kulturbegegnung in parthischer Zeit*. Cologne and Opladen: Westdeutscher Verlag, 1960. First in this author's series of publications that claim an Iranian origin for the *Revelation of the Magi*.

———. *Die Religionen Irans*. Stuttgart: W. Kohlhammer, 1965.

———. *Les religions de l'Iran*. Paris: Payot, 1968.

Bibliography

Witakowski, W. "The Magi in Syriac Tradition." In *Malphono w-Rabo d-Malphone: Studies in Honor of Sebastian P. Brock*, edited by G. A. Kiraz, 809–43. Piscataway, NJ: Gorgias Press, 2008. Examines Syriac interpretations of the Magi story, with special emphasis on the *Revelation of the Magi*.

————. *The Syriac Chronicle of Pseudo-Dionysius of Tel-Mahre: A Study in the History of Historiography*. Uppsala: Uppsala Univ. Press, 1987. Studies the historiographical methods used by the author of the *Chronicle of Zuqnin*.